LIVERPOOL HERITAGE WALK

The Bluecoat Press in association with Liverpool City Council

The Bank of Scotland, in its tercentenary
year, is delighted to assist in the publication
of the Liverpool Heritage Walk

300 YEARS OF
BANKING SERVICE

The **LIVERPOOL HERITAGE WALK** and this
COMPANION GUIDE were devised and produced in
the Liverpool City Planning Department.
Head of Planning & Transportation Service, Chris
Hammer, would like to thank members of the following
organisations for comments and suggestions received:

Liverpool Heritage Bureau.
Merseyside Tourism Board.
Liverpool City Council Promotion and News Unit.

This Guide was written by Philip Browning with
research assistance from John Edwards, a MerseyGuide
with the Merseyside Tourism Board. Typographic
Design by the Graphic Design Unit, Liverpool City
Planning Department.

Illustrations by:
T.G. Conway, J.M. Harrison, C.R. Hutchinson,
S.J. Long, A. Moscardini, G.R. Simons, K. Tan.
Cover illustration by John Thirsk.

ISBN 1 872568 25 4

Published by
The Bluecoat Press
18 Bluecoat Chambers
School Lane
Liverpool L1 3BX

INTRODUCTION

Situated on the east bank of the wide River Mersey, Liverpool city centre occupies one of the most dramatic locations of any British city. The centre is approximately 2.5 square kilometres (one square mile) in size. It runs in a series of plateaux from the waterfront to a ridge to the east, on which two Cathedrals proudly stand. It is acknowledged as one of the most architecturally distinguished central areas in the country.

The city centre is essentially a 19th century creation – earlier development was swept aside by the explosion of economic activity in the Victorian period, when the city was one of the biggest ports in the world. Liverpool, however, has a long history and was established in 1207 when it received its Charter from King John. Growth was slow initially, but by 1551 there was sufficient activity in the river to warrant the appointment of a Water Bailiff to prevent obstruction and congestion.

The 18th century saw the opening of the town's first purpose built dock in 1715 and more were built during that century. Trading with the West Indies, North America, Africa, Europe and other British ports took place at this time, to be followed in the early 19th century by a rapid rise of trade with India and China.

Steam power increased the size of ships and ever larger docks had to be built to accommodate them. The opening of the Liverpool and Manchester Railway in the 1830s heralded the beginning of rail connections to all parts of the country, and the mass movement of goods to and from the port. Samuel Cunard established the first shipping line in 1840 to carry mail and passengers between Liverpool and North America. Further shipping lines were established to convey the increasing number of people, including emigrants, who wished to cross the Atlantic and other oceans of the world.

Liverpool remained a town for nearly 700 years, becoming a city in 1880. Its population reached its zenith in 1931, when 855,000 people were recorded. This figure did not, of course, include the metropolitan area, which had a population of well over a million at that time, as is true today.

Air travel, new trading patterns, and shipping technology have drastically reduced the use of the oldest docks near the city centre. The vast new Royal Seaforth Dock at the mouth of the river, which receives the largest ships, now handles the bulk of shipping in the Mersey. However, the magnificent Georgian and Victorian docks are now ripe for restoration and redevelopment, and many exciting schemes have been completed or are planned, which will further enhance the attractiveness of the centre of Liverpool.

The city's strong links with the rest of the country and all corners of the world have brought about a population with diverse roots. The Celtic inheritance of Scotland, Wales and Ireland has played an important role in Liverpool's development as have the diverse traditions of the Far Eastern, African and Caribbean countries. This mix of people has produced a rich culture which is particularly strong where the arts and sport are concerned. To this must be added a unique sense of humour.

Interest in the city by people in other parts of Britain and the rest of the world has resulted in a rapidly expanding tourist industry. Great efforts are being made by the City Council and other organisations to make sure that the City's heritage, assets and facilities are made known to visitors. This Heritage Walk is but one initiative being undertaken by the City Council to enable the visitor to understand, appreciate and enjoy the centre of this fascinating City.

The Pierhead Trio
Royal Liver Building – Cunard Building – Port of Liverpool Building

HOW TO USE THIS COMPANION GUIDE

The Liverpool Heritage Walk starts and finishes at Lime Street main line station. It has a total distance of 11.5 kilometres (seven miles). It is most unlikely that the walker will undertake the walk in one day due to its length, but will select a section of particular interest to him or her and concentrate on that. Other sections may then be followed later as time permits. This Companion Guide may be read independently of the walk and will still convey much of the fascination of the unique Liverpool City Centre.

Seventy five gun metal 'Markers', 177 mm (7″) square, have been set into street footways and pedestrian areas and are numbered 1 to 75. The city centre map following this section shows the full extent of the walk and the sequence of the markers. Each double page spread describing the walk includes a map showing the exact location of each marker covered on the double page.

The maps also show the locations of City of Liverpool plaques. These have been erected on walls and buildings on the advice of the Liverpool Heritage Bureau. The red plaques record buildings and sites associated with historical events and notable persons. The blue plaques indicate buildings of architectural merit and the green plaques record the sites of demolished buildings.

At the back of this Companion Guide may be found a list of useful addresses of interest to the visitor.

The following breakdown of the walk gives an indication of the character of the various sections of it, to enable the walker to select the stretch he or she wishes to follow.

MARKERS

1 to 4 Gilded palaces and public houses.
St George's Hall; Lime Street; two Edwardian public houses; Britain's 'front door'.

4 to 6 Red brick ascent to the Georgian town.
A city centre garden; a Spanish writer; enterprising Scots; the first U.S. Consul in the world; a great Liverpool architect.

6 to 13 Two cathedrals linked by Hope Street.
The Roman Catholic cathedral; one of Liverpool's most eminent sons; links with South Carolina; macabre events in a cellar; the most lavish public house in Britain; a Beatles' school and college; the Anglican cathedral.

13 to 18 An elegant street and eminent persons.
Rodney Street; a member of the Bloomsbury Group; a Liverpool photographer; a talented poet and a feminist; the birthplace of a prime minister; the first Medical Officer of Health; an author; a great electrical engineer.

18 to 20 Chinatown.
Scandinavian refuge; 'The Inn of the Sixth Happiness'; the first Chinese settlement in Europe; a benefactor from China; the father of orthopaedics; the industrial world's first public washing facilities.

20 to 23 Pens, paints and pistols in a merchants' street.
Early Liverpool housing; an American author and consul; the author of 'The boy stood on the burning deck . . .'; the last duel in Liverpool; the man who shot a prime minister; a painter of royalty.

23 to 25 Yo, ho, ho and a bottle of rum.
The Pool of Liverpool; Paradise Street; a sea shanty; 'Poor Mercantile Jack'; Liverpool's first dock.

25 to 28 Gargantuan docks of the age of sail.
The 'Press Gang'; Albert Dock; a great dock engineer; mouth of the Pool; the 'Dockers' Umbrella'; a double VC.

28 to 36 Threshold to the ends of the earth.
The slave trade; history of the Mersey; Merchant Navy memorial; Liverpool Trades Council podium; Port of Liverpool building; Belgian Merchant Navy plaque; early steamships; the Cunard Building and the Cunard Line; the Royal Liver Building; the Liver Bird; an American memorial stone; American G.I.s; where the liners tied up; 'Titanic Memorial'; Tower of Liverpool.

36 to 40 Victorian finery on a mediaeval foundation.
The White Star Line; the inventor of 'Meccano'; Liverpool Castle; the Civil War; the Victoria Monument; architectural riches; the Sanctuary Stone; the seven original mediaeval streets.

40 to 45 Palaces of the merchant princes.
The Town Hall; Beatlemania; Liverpool Insurance; well-dressed Victorian gentlemen; boxes of gold; two important telephone kiosks; a great national hero; palaces of commerce; a pioneering building; a young American visitor.

45 to 49 Church, citadel and Confederate cause.
Privateering; St Nicholas's Church; two great Liverpudlians; Combined Headquarters of the Western Approaches; Confederate Embassy in England.

49 to 53 Kingdom of cotton.
Two Liverpool companies; the Cotton Exchange; the composer of 'Amazing Grace'; a building for the cotton trade; George Stubbs' birthplace; Britain's football pool centre.

53 to 55 Mediaeval lanes.
Mayors and Lord Mayors of Liverpool; Liverpool's Coat of Arms; Hackins Hey; early Quaker buildings.

55 to 59 Commercial pomp and civic pride.
Commercial and municipal chambers; former street of stage coaches and hostelries; the good Saint; cast iron churches for export; an American patriot.

59 to 62 Victorian hive of trade and commerce.
A handsome railway goods office; Liverpool comedians; a French prince and the author of 'Vanity Fair'; a bronze Eleanor Rigby; a new Victorian street; smoked fish and the Salvation Army; an early glass building.

62 to 63 In the footsteps of the Beatles.
The Cavern Club; a new building recalling the Beatles; sculpture by Cynthia Lennon, John Doubleday and Arthur Dooley; a gorilla applying lipstick.

63 to 64 The Pool of Liverpool.
The line of the Pool; the origin of the name 'Liverpool'; Brian Epstein.

64 to 70 Shops, shops and more shops.
The first Woolworth's in Europe; Bluecoat Chambers; the
Brooks family; the Lyceum; a lady of taste; the man who
assassinated President Lincoln; Britain's oldest repertory
theatre company; Richard Burton's first public
appearance; the south front of St George's Hall.

70 to 75 Temples of culture.
French prisoners of war; a dynasty of social reformers; the
Mersey Tunnel; museum, libraries and art galleries; a
Column with a twin in Edinburgh; avoiding the 'Window
Tax'; the Cenotaph; a vigil for John Lennon; a
controversial statue; the last performance of the Beatles in
Liverpool; a handsome hotel.

Markers 25 & 26 are within the Albert Dock Estate which is
private property owned and managed by Merseyside
Development Corporation. Access to the Estate is usually
available between 10 a.m. and Midnight each day except
Christmas Day.

The Town Hall with the Royal Liver Building in the background

5

Liverpool City Centre

Scale
0   ¼ Km   ¼ mile

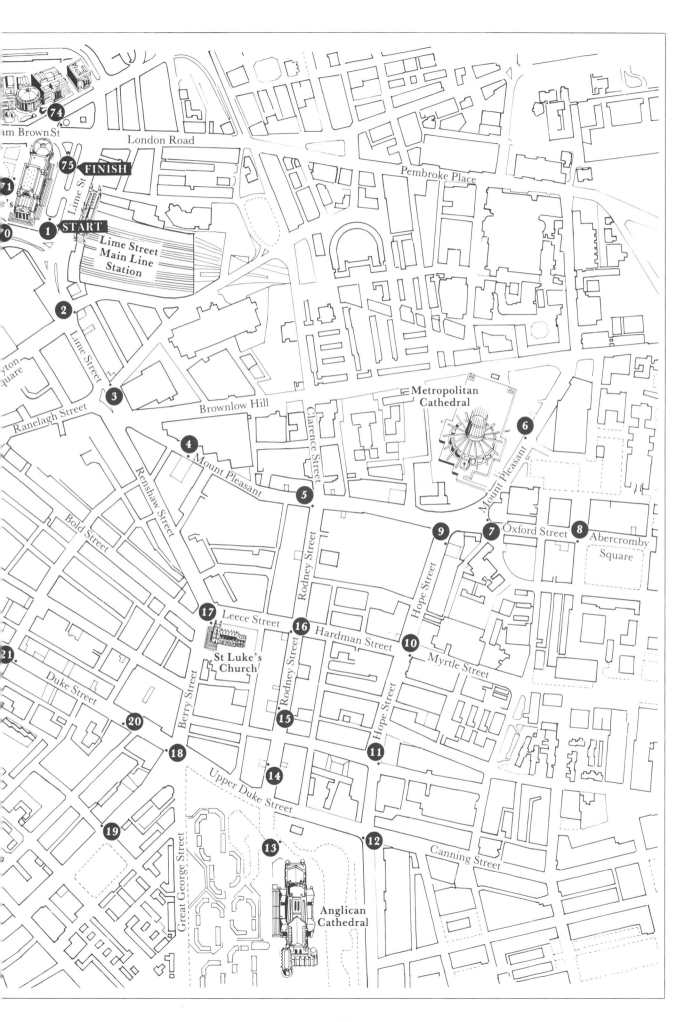

74

am Brown St

London Road

75 **FINISH**

Pembroke Place

Lime St

71

e's

0

START

Lime Street Main Line Station

2

Lime Street

3

Brownlow Hill

Clarence Street

Metropolitan Cathedral

6

Mount Pleasant

Ranelagh Street

4

Mount Pleasant

5

7 Oxford Street 8

Abercromby

Square

yton quare

Renshaw Street

Bold Street

Rodney Street

9

Hope Street

Duke Street

21

17 Leece Street

16 Hardman Street

10 Myrtle Street

Berry Street

St Luke's Church

Rodney Street

20

15

Hope Street

18

11

14

Upper Duke Street

19

Great George Street

13

12 Canning Street

Anglican Cathedral

7

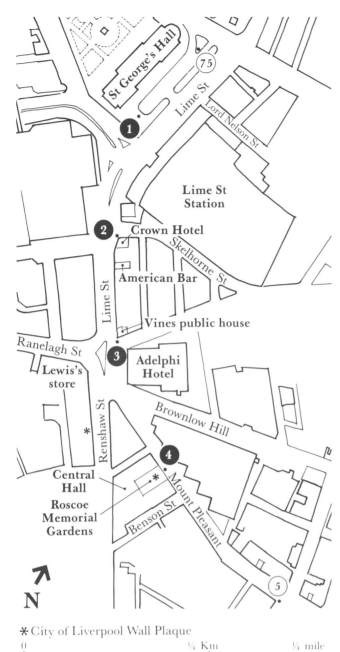

Harvey Lonsdale Elmes

journeying from London to Liverpool, began to take its toll. At 30 years of age he contracted tuberculosis and three years later, in 1847, he died whilst undertaking a cure in Jamaica. The hall was only half finished.

Professor C R Cockerell, his mentor and family friend, was brought in to finish the building. It was opened by the Mayor in 1854. The interior is Roman in derivation and much of the exterior is pure Greek. It is considered one of the greatest neo-classical buildings in the world and **Queen Victoria** said that it was *'Worthy of Ancient Athens'.*

The building has a notable interior. The main room is the Great Hall which is 52 metres (169') long and 25.5 metres (84') high. It has a sumptuous Minton tile floor and much fine sculpture and plasterwork. The second principal room is the Small Concert Hall which was designed by Professor C R Cockerell. It is considered one of the finest

St George's Hall

interiors of the early Victorian period. This room, with its maidens supporting the balcony, its mirrors and a large chandelier, is magical and was used by Charles Dickens for many of his *'Readings'.* There are also two grand Court rooms incorporating much marble and fine plasterwork.

The Courts have witnessed many interesting trials, the two most sensational being those of **Mrs Maybrick** and **Mr Wallace.** In 1889 Florence Maybrick, the daughter of an American banker, was convicted of poisoning her wealthy Liverpool cotton broker husband James. Although convicted, she was not executed but imprisoned for 15 years and then freed. In 1931 William Herbert Wallace was firstly convicted, and then on appeal acquitted, of the brutal murder of his wife, Julia. There was, and still is, controversy as to who did commit each crime.

See Marker 70 for the South Facade of St George's Hall. See Marker 75 for St George's Plateau, its sculpture and adjacent buildings.

ST GEORGE'S HALL.

The site of **St George's Hall** was, from 1749 to 1824, occupied by the first Liverpool Infirmary which also incorporated a Seaman's Hospital, Medical Library and a Lunatic Asylum. The Seaman's Hospital was mainly supported by a levy of sixpence a month, which was deducted from the pay of seamen sailing in ships registered in Liverpool.

In 1836 it was decided that Liverpool needed new premises to house the four day musical festival that took place in the town every three years. A competition for a concert hall design was eventually held, which was won by a 23 year old London architect, **Harvey Lonsdale Elmes (1814-1847).** The town next decided to hold a second competition for Assize Courts which was also won by Elmes. The Corporation then decided to combine the two schemes and Elmes produced a design.

Work started on St George's Hall in 1842 and Elmes superintended the work. He was a frail man and the responsibility for the project, coupled with the constant

LIME STREET, LIME STREET STATION.

Lime Street until 1790 was known as Lime Kiln Lane. It was named after William Harvey's kilns which stood near the present Lord Nelson Street north of the railway station. In 1804 doctors at the infirmary, situated where St

George's Hall now stands, objected to the fumes from the kilns and after litigation the kilns were relocated elsewhere.

From the beginning of the 19th century, Lime Street was known for the *'Ladies of the Night'* who paraded along it. The most famous was *'Maggie May'*, who was immortalised in the popular song of the same name.

The site of **Lime Street station** became the western terminus of the Liverpool and Manchester Railway in 1836. The first building complex was erected on the site in that year to be followed by a second one in 1851. The third station was started in 1867 and included the present northern *'train shed'* which was then the largest in the world with a span of 61 metres (200′).

The **Liverpool and Manchester Railway** was opened in 1830. In addition to carrying *'goods only'* trains, it was the first railway with fast steam locomotives running to a regular passenger timetable. It was a pioneer of modern railway operation and was 49 kilometres (31 miles) long. It ran initially into Crown Street near Edge Hill in inner Liverpool. In 1836 the line was extended by tunnel to Lime Street and trains descended into the station by gravity, being hauled back to Edge Hill by an endless cable. In 1870 improved tunnel size and ventilation enabled locomotives to take over.

Just north of Skelhorne Street on Lime Street was the location, in the 19th century, of **Josephine Butler's night shelter for women. Josephine Butler (1828-1906)** came to Liverpool in 1866 and campaigned courageously against the Contagious Diseases Acts. She established refuges for destitute and ill prostitutes and opened a training centre to offer an alternative to prostitution. In addition she worked tirelessly for education for women and in the women's suffrage campaigns.

The **Crown Hotel,** completed in 1905, is a rich confection of brick, glass and copper externally, with sumptuous plasterwork and marble internally. It is one of the most exuberant *'art nouveau'* public houses in Liverpool.

The **American Bar** on the east side of Lime Street was, until the 1920s, on the other side of the street and was established in the 1830s. The bar, which has objects and memorabilia associated with the **United States,** was well used by US sailors, soldiers and airmen during the First and Second World Wars.

ADELPHI HOTEL; BARON RIO BRANCO; DAVID LEWIS.

The fine, Edwardian, **Vines public house** was completed in 1907 and was designed by **Walter Thomas,** the brewery architect. It has a sumptuous interior of mahogany, beaten copper and rich plasterwork. Particularly good is the rear salon which was originally designed for billiards. This famous public house is known in Liverpool as the *'Big House'*.

The street junction in front of the Adelphi Hotel is called **Ranelagh Place.** The hotel and Ranelagh Street take their name from a pavilion and tea garden, which were from 1722 to 1790 located on the site of the hotel. The present **Adelphi Hotel,** the second on the site, was designed by **Frank Atkinson.** It was built to accommodate the wealthy passengers *'overnighting'* before and after a transatlantic trip. When completed in 1912 it was considered one of the most luxurious in the world. It was known as Britain's *'front door'* and kings, queens, princes, presidents and prime ministers have stayed there. It is also famous for its international parties on Grand National Night.

In 1954 **Roy Rogers** was a guest, and rode his horse **Trigger** up the front steps and into the hotel. Trigger later appeared at a first floor window to the delight of a large crowd below.

Brazil has had strong links with Liverpool for many years. The **Baron Rio Branco (1846-1912),** one of

Brazil's greatest statesmen, made his home in the first Adelphi Hotel as Consul General from 1877 until 1892. In the year of the Declaration of Independence from Portugal in 1822, Brazil's first overseas Consulate worldwide was established in Liverpool, reflecting the vital importance of trading links with this city which date back to the 16th century.

Adelphi Hotel

Lewis's store opposite was badly bombed in the last war and has been largely rebuilt. The large statue by **Jacob Epstein** over the main entrance was unveiled in 1957. Entitled *'Liverpool Resurgent'*, it symbolises the resurgence of Liverpool after the blitz. **David Lewis** founded Lewis's in Liverpool in 1856 and since that time branches have been opened in several cities in Britain.

The store occupies the site of the former **Renshaw Street workshop** of **Peter Litherland (1756-1804),** who invented and patented the rack lever escapement for watches. Part of Lewis's also occupies the site of the former **German Lutheran Chapel,** which served the German community in Liverpool until it was demolished in the 1950s. Many **Germans** came to Liverpool as seamen but a sizeable number also owned or worked in pork butcher's shops.

ROSCOE MEMORIAL GARDENS; JOSEPH BLANCO WHITE.

The **Roscoe Memorial Gardens** were once the burial ground of the old **Renshaw Street Unitarian Chapel,** which used to stand where the Central Hall is now located. **William Roscoe (1753-1831),** one of Liverpool's most illustrious sons, was buried here, hence the name of the gardens. He worshipped at the Chapel and was born at the top of Mount Pleasant. The monument in the middle of the gardens with its eight Doric columns commemorates the chapel which was built in 1811.

Also buried in the former burial ground was **Joseph Blanco White (1775-1846).** He was born Don José Maria

Joseph Blanco White

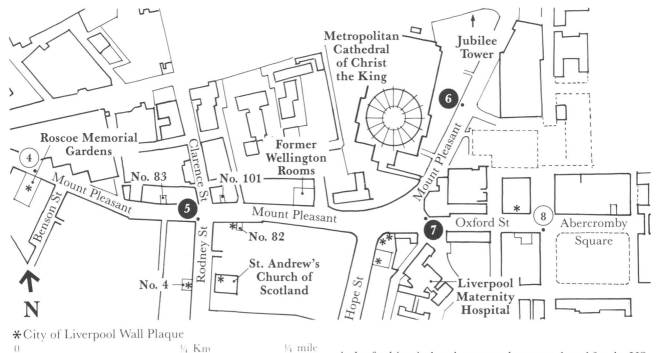

Scale

circles for his wind and current charts produced for the US Navy.

Blanco y Crespo in Seville of prosperous **Spanish** parents who were strict Roman Catholics. He was ordained as a priest and was set to follow an illustrious career in the church when doubts set in. When the French marched into Madrid in 1808 he fled to England. He lived in London, Oxford and Dublin before coming to Liverpool, where he spent the last six years of his life.

When in London, White left the Roman Catholic church and became an Anglican. Well known as a religious thinker and political journalist, he was a poet in both English and Spanish. On arriving in Liverpool, he became friendly with the many prominent Unitarians in the town, who were prosperous, influential and cultured. He continued to write in Liverpool. After his health failed he was nursed for the last few weeks of his life by the Rathbone family at Greenbank, their home near Mossley Hill.

JAMES MAURY; JOHN FOSTER JUNIOR; BRANDON THOMAS.

Many enterprising **Scots** came to Liverpool in the 18th and 19th centuries and became involved in such activities as ship building, rope making, engineering and sugar refining. **Laird** established a foundry and ship building empire and other entrepreneurs built Scottish kirks including **St Andrew's Church of Scotland** in Rodney Street in 1823. It was designed by **John Foster junior** and is situated a few steps south of here on the east side of Rodney Street. In the churchyard is a monument in the form of a pyramid to **W. Mackenzie** which was built in 1868. Mackenzie was a railway contractor and reputed to have been an avid gambler. Folklore has it that he wished to be buried sitting upright at a card table with a winning hand, hence the pyramid.

No. 4 Rodney Street was the residence of **James Maury (1746-1840),** the first United States Consul in Liverpool and indeed anywhere in the world. He was the **American** Consul in Liverpool from 1790 to 1829 and was personally appointed by George Washington. He was a classmate of Thomas Jefferson and his portrait hangs in Liverpool Town Hall. James Maury's son, **Lieutenant Maury USN,** who was born in Liverpool, is well known in American naval

James Maury

Trade with America at the beginning of the 19th century was so great that the American Chamber of Commerce set up a branch in Liverpool in 1801 which lasted for 100 years. Liverpool was so well known in the United States that six settlements there were named after the town.

Part of Liverpool Polytechnic occupies most of the south side of Mount Pleasant between Rodney Street and Hope Street. The complex occupies the site of **No. 82 Mount Pleasant,** which was originally the home of **John Foster junior (c. 1786-1846).** He was one of Liverpool's greatest architects and was Corporation Surveyor from 1824 to 1835. He undertook the Grand Tour in the early 19th century visiting Italy and Greece. He worked on excavations in Greece with **Professor C R Cockerell** who called him — *"A most amazing youth, but too idle to be anything more than a dinner companion".* Foster undertook at least 18 large commissions in and around Liverpool, and so must have overcome his youthful inertia.

View down Mount Pleasant

Brandon Thomas (1856-1914) the dramatist, was born at No. 101 Mount Pleasant and later lived at No. 83 Mount Pleasant. He was a Merseyside shipyard worker, but later became a journalist in Liverpool and also an author. In the 1890s he wrote the play 'Charley's Aunt'.

The Wellington Rooms, now the Irish Centre, were opened in 1816. The building was designed by Edmund Aiken and built as fashionable subscription assembly rooms for the Wellington Club.

R.C. METROPOLITAN CATHEDRAL: LIVERPOOL WORKHOUSE: LIVERPOOL UNIVERSITY.

The site of the Metropolitan Cathedral of Christ the King was bought in 1930 by the Roman Catholic authorities, who commissioned Sir Edwin Lutyens (1869-1944) to design a cathedral. Sir Edwin was the architect of such works as the Cenotaph in Whitehall and Viceroy's House in New Delhi. His proposed cathedral in Liverpool incorporated a dome 51 metres (168') in diameter and 158 metres (520') high from the ground. The building was to be larger than St Peter's in Rome. The foundation stone was laid in 1933 and part of the crypt was constructed. Work had to stop in 1940 due to the Second World War.

In 1952 Lutyens' scheme was calculated to cost £27 million and efforts were made to modify the scheme to reduce the cost. They came to nothing and in 1959 a design competition was held for a new cathedral to incorporate Lutyens' crypt. Sir Frederick Gibberd (1908-1984) won the competition with the present design, which took four and a half years to build and cost £1.9 million. It was consecrated and opened in 1967.

The building has an internal diameter of 59 metres (194'), a height of 78 metres (255') and space for 2,200 worshippers. The altar is of Yugoslavian marble and the total weight of the bells is 10.2 tonnes (10 tons). The building contains works by many contemporary artists of whom John Piper, Patrick Reyntiens, Elizabeth Frink and Ceri Richards are notable. Pope John Paul II attended a service at the Metropolitan Cathedral on the 30th May 1982 after he had attended a previous service at the Anglican Cathedral.

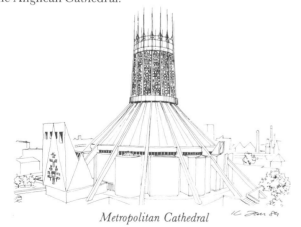

Metropolitan Cathedral

In the 19th century the site of the Metropolitan Cathedral was occupied by one of the largest workhouses in England capable of housing up to 5,000 people. At this time Liverpool was a magnet for many people not only looking for work, but arriving in the Port as the first stage to a new and hopefully better life overseas. In 1847 alone, 300,000 desperately poor Irish disembarked in Liverpool from heavily overloaded boats after the failure of the Irish potato crop in 1845 and 1846. Many would have spent at least some time in the workhouse, if not their last days there.

The problem of poverty and destitution remained and in 1865 William Rathbone became increasingly concerned about the conditions of the sick in the workhouse. He funded the introduction of a proper nursing system and wrote and asked Agnes Jones (1832-1868) to take charge. Born in Cambridge, Agnes Jones had trained as a nurse under Florence Nightingale. She came to Liverpool with approximately 50 nurses for 1,500 patients and revolutionised the care of sick paupers. In 1868, aged 35, she caught typhoid fever and died.

The Jubilee Tower of the Victoria Building of Liverpool University rises to the north and was completed in 1892. It was designed by Alfred Waterhouse (1830-1905), and contains a chiming clock. The clock was paid for by William Pickles Hartley, the Liverpool jam and marmalade manufacturer.

WILLIAM ROSCOE; JOHN LENNON.

In this area, in the 18th century, stood the 'Bowling Green Inn' where William Roscoe (1753-1831), one of Liverpool's most eminent sons, spent his childhood. His father kept the inn and also a market garden, and his son helped him grow and sell the produce. William Roscoe's schooling was indifferent but his mother bought him books and taught him piety.

William Roscoe

Aged 16, he was articled to a solicitor. He became attached to a group of young intellectuals and taught himself Latin, Greek, French and Italian and was addicted to English poetry. He was keen for Liverpool to follow the example of the small Italian city states of the Middle Ages which used their prosperity to promote art and learning.

He helped form a society to encourage designing, drawing and painting and from this emerged the 'Liverpool Academy for the Encouragement of Fine Arts'. At the same time he began his collection of prints and Italian paintings. A life long member of the Unitarian congregation, he was greatly concerned with abolishing the slave trade. In 1806 he briefly became M.P. for one of the two Liverpool seats, and saw through a Bill for the abolition of the slave trade.

Much of Roscoe's wealth was due to his activities as a lawyer and later a banker. He had a happy marriage and a large family. In 1795 he completed 'The Life of Lorenzo de Medici' which won universal acclaim both in Britain and abroad. The book was printed and published in Liverpool as he wished to control production and also establish Liverpool as a literary centre.

The bank in which he was a partner failed, and between 1816 and 1820 he had to sell his possessions. His books went to the Athenaeum Club and his paintings to the Royal Institution in Liverpool which he had helped to found. Friends rallied to his defence and helped him financially, and he ended his life in intellectual contemplation in Lodge Lane not far from the city centre.

Looking south is Liverpool Maternity Hospital where John Lennon was born on 9th October 1940.

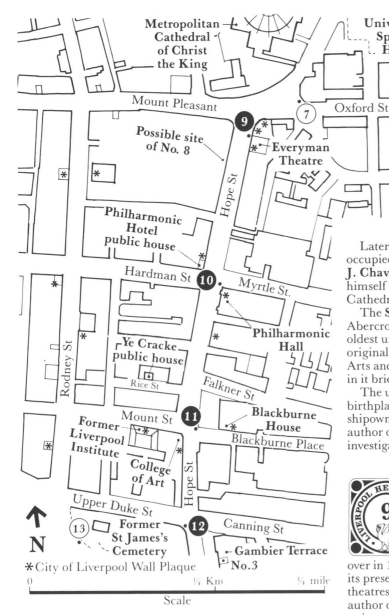

Metropolitan Cathedral of Christ the King

Mount Pleasant

University Sports Hall

School of Architecture

No.19

Oxford St

Abercromby Square

Possible site of No. 8

Everyman Theatre

Hope St

Philharmonic Hotel public house

Hardman St

Myrtle St.

Philharmonic Hall

Rodney St

Ye Cracke public house

Rice St

Falkner St.

Mount St

Blackburne House

Blackburne Place

Former Liverpool Institute

College of Art

Hope St

Upper Duke St

N

Former St James's Cemetery

Canning St

Gambier Terrace No.3

*City of Liverpool Wall Plaque

0   ¼ Km   ¼ mile

Scale

ABERCROMBY SQUARE; C. K. PRIOLEAU; FRANCIS J. CHAVASSE; AUGUSTUS JOHN; CHARLES BOOTH

The handsome **Abercromby Square** was named after **Sir Ralph Abercromby.** He was an intrepid general who was killed in Alexandria in 1801 after his brilliant landing of the British forces at Aboukir, Egypt.

No. 19 Abercromby Square was originally built for **C. K. Prioleau,** an agent of the **Confederate government.** Above the front door fanlight the stonework bears the *'Bonnie Blue'* stars of **South Carolina** immortalised in the southern song *'The Bonnie Blue Flag'.* The entrance columns also sport 'Bonnie Blues', and on the ceiling inside the doorway may be found the Palmetto Tree, the state tree of South Carolina.

Abercromby Square

Later No. 19 became the **Bishop's Palace,** which was occupied between 1900 and 1923 by the **Rt Revd. Francis J. Chavasse (1846-1928),** the Bishop of Liverpool. He set himself the task of beginning the building of an Anglican Cathedral for Liverpool.

The **School of Architecture,** now housed in Abercromby Square, was established in 1895 and is the oldest university School of Architecture in Britain. It was originally set up as a School of Architecture and Applied Arts and **Augustus John (1878-1961),** the painter, taught in it briefly in the early 1900s.

The university **Sports Hall** incorporates the site of the birthplace of **Charles Booth (1840-1916),** a Liverpool shipowner and pioneer of social research. He was the author of *'Life and Labour of the People in London',* which he investigated in the 1890s.

EVERYMAN THEATRE; THE CELLAR OF No. 8 HOPE STREET.

The **Everyman Theatre** started life in the 1830s as a Revivalist Preaching House. The **Everyman Company** took it over in 1964, after which it was extensively rebuilt to fulfil its present role as one of Britain's foremost repertory theatres. The Liverpool playwrights **Willy Russell,** the author of *'Educating Rita',* and **Alan Bleasdale,** have both written plays for the theatre.

It is difficult to exactly identify **No. 8 Hope Street** in the early 19th century due to the renumbering of the street, but it could have been located where the Polytechnic building now stands. No 8 was originally a dwelling house owned in the year 1826 by a **Revd James Macgowen.** He let his cellar to a **Mr John Henderson,** a native of Greenock in Scotland, who claimed to be an exporter of fish oil. His real occupation, however, was somewhat different.

One dark October night in 1826, three large oil casks were delivered to a ship waiting to sail for Leith, Edinburgh from the Pier Head area. The next morning sailors were so overcome by the stench from the barrels that they asked the captain to investigate. He was horrified to find that the barrels contained no less than 11 human bodies packed in salt. The man who delivered the casks was traced, and he took the authorities to No 8 Hope Street. The cellar door was broken down to reveal a scene of unimaginable horror. Scattered around in sacks and barrels were the corpses of 22 men, women and children. It was a body snatcher's warehouse!

October was the month when anatomical lectures were beginning in Scottish medical schools, and Scottish churchyards were so well guarded that anatomists turned to England. Corpses were exhumed in Liverpool and brought to No. 8 Hope Street for *'suitable'* packaging and despatch. Henderson, the supposed exporter of fish oil, fled before he was caught and was never found.

PHILHARMONIC HOTEL;
PHILHARMONIC HALL;
EDWARD FALKNER;
YE CRACKE PUBLIC HOUSE.

The **Philharmonic Hotel public house** is reputed to be the most lavish in Britain. Its sumptuous *'gin palace'* interior utilises mahogany, copper, plaster and stained glass to great effect. It was designed by **Walter Thomas,** the brewery architect, and was completed in 1900. Artists and craftsmen from Liverpool University's School of Architecture and Applied Arts were fully involved. **Blomfield Bare's** work on the copper panels and iron and copper entrance gates is particularly notable.

Philharmonic Hotel Entrance Gates

A former **Philharmonic Hall** was completed in 1849 and stood on the site of the present building until it was burnt down in 1933. Like its successor it was noted for its fine acoustics. The present building, the home of the **Royal Liverpool Philharmonic Society,** was designed in the Dutch expressionist style of Wilhelm Dudok by the Liverpool architect, **Herbert Rowse (1887-1963).** It was completed in 1939. The Philharmonic Society, which was founded in 1840, is the only such society in the United Kingdom whose national orchestra has its own hall.

Sir Adrian Boult, born in 1889, was the son of a Liverpool import merchant who was connected with the Philharmonic Society. He was the youngest ever conductor in 1916. **Sir Malcolm Sargent** was the principal conductor of the orchestra from 1942 till 1948.

A few steps south is **Falkner Street.** It was originally called Crabtree Lane, but was renamed after **Edward Falkner.** He enrolled a thousand men in one hour for the defence of Liverpool in 1797, when a French invasion was threatened.

Ye Cracke public house in Rice Street has been patronised by Liverpool art students from the adjacent art school for many years. **John Lennon** was a frequent visitor with his cronies, and his tutorials were often conducted in a back room. It was here that John Lennon's romance blossomed with **Cynthia Powell** who became his first wife.

BLACKBURNE HOUSE; LIVERPOOL INSTITUTE; COLLEGE OF ART.

This area in the 18th century was a peat bog known as **Mosslake Fields.** In 1800 **John Foster senior** prepared a grid iron street plan for it, linking the houses then springing up on Mount Pleasant and Rodney Street.

Blackburne House was built in the open countryside in c. 1785-90 as a detached mansion for **John Blackburne** who was Mayor of Liverpool in 1788. The surviving portion of the Georgian house has a curved bow to the rear and an elegant portico over a double entrance stairway on to Blackburne Place. In 1844 **George Holt,** of the Liverpool shipowning family, founded the first girls' day grammar school in this building.

Down Mount Street is the former **Liverpool Institute,** a well known school which closed in the mid-1980s. It was built as the Mechanics' Institution and opened in 1837. **Mark Twain (1835-1910),** the **American** novelist and humourist, lectured here and included in the audience was **Silas K. Hocking (1850-1935),** a Liverpool Methodist Minister. In 1879 he wrote a *'best seller'* on Liverpool waifs entitled *'Her Benny'.* **Charles Dickens** also gave readings here.

Many interesting people attended the Liverpool Institute, including **R. J. Lloyd (1846-1906),** a promoter of Esperanto (the international language), in its early stages, and also a phonetic alphabet. **J. E. Wright (1878-1910),** who became a Professor of Mathematics at Princeton, U.S.A., also attended. Old boys include **Arthur Askey,** the comedian; **Maxwell Fry,** one of the pioneers of modern architecture in Britain; **Edward Halliday,** the painter; and **Paul McCartney** and **George Harrison.**

The **College of Art building,** completed in 1910, was designed by **Willink and Thicknesse,** the architects of the Cunard Building. **John Lennon** attended the college between 1957 and 1959.

GAMBIER TERRACE;
ST JAMES'S CEMETERY;
THE RT HON WILLIAM HUSKISSON,
M.P.; ANDREW CARNEGIE

Gambier Terrace is an elegant terrace of stucco houses constructed between 1832-7, probably to a design of **John Foster junior. John Lennon** in his early days as a student shared a flat at No. 3 Gambier Terrace.

Gambier Terrace

The deep hollow to the south was originally a stone quarry, but opened as **St James's Cemetery** in 1829 to a design of **John Foster junior.** Note the intersecting sloping carriageways with retaining walls containing catacombs, which were part of the cemetery design. Between 1829 and its closure in 1936 57,774 bodies were interred here, including those of **Kitty Wilkinson,** the pioneer of public baths and wash houses in Liverpool, **Sir William Brown,** who paid for the Brown Library, **Captain William Harrison** who commanded the *'Great Eastern'* and **Captain John Oliver,** a veteran of the Battles of the Nile, Copenhagen and Trafalgar, He served on H.M.S. *'Victory'* under Admiral Lord Nelson and died at the age of 102 in 1876.

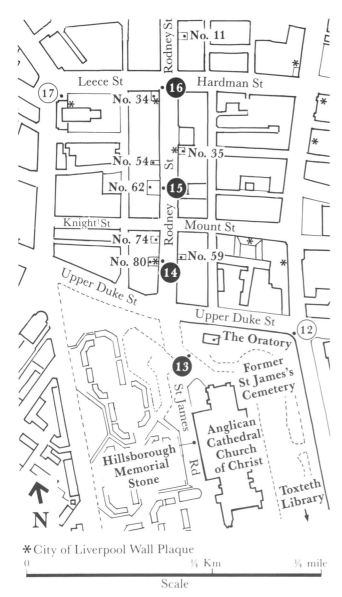

No. 11
Rodney St
Leece St   Hardman St
(17)   No. 34   16
No. 54   No. 35
No. 62   15
Knight St   Rodney St   Mount St
No. 74   No. 59
No. 80   14
Upper Duke St
Upper Duke St
(12)
The Oratory
13   Former St James's Cemetery
St James Rd
Anglican Cathedral Church of Christ
Hillsborough Memorial Stone   Toxteth Library
N

✱ City of Liverpool Wall Plaque

0   ¼ Km   ¼ mile

Scale

103 entries were sent in and the 21 year old Giles Gilbert Scott won it. The design originally had twin towers but this was later changed to one. The building is constructed of local sandstone in a free Gothic style.

The foundation stone was laid by **H. M. King Edward VII** in 1904 and **H. M. Queen Elizabeth II** attended a Service of Thanksgiving for its completion in 1978. Work continued through both world wars and at one time 300 masons were employed on site. The Lady Chapel was the first to be completed in 1910, the tower was finished by 1942 and the nave at the northern end (liturgical west end) finished in time for the completion ceremonies.

Anglican Cathedral

The building holds a number of records. It is the largest Anglican Cathedral in the world with the highest Gothic arches and vaults ever built. The organ with nearly 10,000 pipes is the biggest to be found in any church, and the cathedral has the highest and heaviest ringing peal of bells in the world. The tower is 100 metres (331') high above St James Road.

Fine sculpture can be found both inside and outside the cathedral. This is almost entirely the work of **Edward Carter Preston (1885-1965),** the superb Liverpool sculptor. Most of his cathedral sculpture has faces based on his relatives and friends and he was also responsible for most of the memorial wall plaques. Early on in the reign of H.M. Queen Elizabeth II, he designed her personal Duchy of Lancaster seal incorporating Her Majesty, her horse and her favourite corgi, the latter at her special request. Inside the cathedral try to find the monkey attempting to distort the scales of justice!

The architect, Sir Giles Gilbert Scott, who was a Roman Catholic, was buried with his wife outside the Cathedral just north of the liturgical West Door. The architect of the Roman Catholic Metropolitan Cathedral, Sir Frederick Gibberd, was a Congregationalist!

At the front of the Rankin Porch steps is the **Hillsborough Memorial Stone.** On the 15th April, 1989, Liverpool Football Club was playing Nottingham Forest in a F.A. Cup semi-final at Hillsborough football ground in Sheffield. At the beginning of the match many Liverpool fans lost their lives or were injured due to overcrowding in sections of a spectators' stand.

During the week following the disaster, over a million people visited Liverpool's ground at Anfield, leaving a vast sea of flowers there as a tribute to the 95 who lost their lives. Supporters of Everton, the City's other football club, and Tranmere Rovers based in Birkenhead, lent their support during this tragic time. Leading national and local figures and representatives of all Merseyside's churches attended a great service of remembrance in the Anglican Cathedral on the 29th April, 1989, after which the Memorial Stone was hallowed and wreaths were laid.

Spectacularly sited by the Cathedral is '**The Oratory**'. Originally the mortuary chapel for St James's Cemetery, it

The most famous grave is that of the **Rt Hon William Huskisson, M.P. (1770-1830).** He was killed by **Stephenson's** *'Rocket',* at Parkside in Lancashire at the opening of the Liverpool and Manchester Railway in 1830. Crossing the line to speak to the Duke of Wellington in another carriage, he was struck by the oncoming *'Rocket'* which severed one of his legs and he died later in the day. His grave is marked by a domed rotunda designed by **John Foster junior.**

The cemetery is now a public park and at its southern end the twin red brick gables of the **Toxteth Library** may be glimpsed. This building, together with four other Liverpool branch libraries, was paid for by the **American** steel magnate and philanthropist **Andrew Carnegie,** who was of **Scottish** descent. Mr Carnegie came to Liverpool in 1902 to open the library personally. It was designed by **Thomas Shelmerdine,** the Corporation Surveyor.

ANGLICAN CATHEDRAL; 'THE ORATORY'.

The **Anglican Cathedral Church of Christ** is orientated north to south, rather than the customary east to west, to take advantage of its spectacular site overlooking the city centre. The cathedral today is a radically different design from the one submitted by the architect **(Sir) Giles Gilbert Scott (1880-1960)** for the Cathedral Competition held in 1901.

takes the form of a miniature Greek Doric Temple. It was designed by **John Foster junior** and completed in 1829. It is considered one of Foster's greatest works.

LYTTON STRACHEY; E. CHAMBRÉ HARDMAN; ARTHUR CLOUGH; ANNE CLOUGH.

Rodney Street was first proposed shortly after Lord Rodney's 1782 naval victory over the Comte de Grasse. It was one of several new residential areas springing up on the outskirts of the town at this time. By 1801 it appears that most of the street had been developed.

Lytton Strachey (1880-1932), taught for a time at Liverpool University and lived at **No. 80 Rodney Street.** He was a member of the Bloomsbury Group of authors and artists and his books include *'Queen Victoria'* and *'Eminent Victorians'.*

No. 59 opposite was the home and studio, until his death, of **E. Chambré Hardman (1898-1988),** the Liverpool photographer. He was a photographer of distinction and his commercial work is an important part of British photographic history. His greatest work is considered to be the launch of an aircraft carrier at Birkenhead entitled *'The Birth of the Ark Royal'.*

Arthur Hugh Clough (1819-1861), was born at **No. 74 Rodney Street.** Clough was the son of a Liverpool cotton merchant and became Principal of University Hall, University College, London. He was a poet of distinction and during the Second World War, Winston Churchill quoted a piece of his poetry on the radio.

Arthur Clough's sister, **Anne Jemima Clough (1820-1892),** was also born at No. 74. She was an educationalist and feminist. She was a trained teacher and joined forces with Josephine Butler, the wife of the headmaster of Liverpool College, in a campaign to open universities up to women. She took charge of the first house for women students in Cambridge, which became Newnham College, in 1880.

WILLIAM EWART GLADSTONE; DR. W. H. DUNCAN.

John Gladstones (1764-1851), came as a youth from Leith, near Edinburgh to Liverpool in 1787. From humble beginnings, he made a fortune out of commerce with America, the West Indies and India. It was to India that he sent the first Liverpool vessel in 1814. He changed his name in 1837 from Gladstones to Gladstone.

His son **William Ewart Gladstone (1809-1898),** the fifth of six children, was born at what is now **No. 62 Rodney Street.** William Gladstone spent his early years at

William Ewart Gladstone

the family home in Seaforth just north of Liverpool. In 1821 he went to Eton and then in 1828 to Christ Church, Oxford where he gained a double first class honours degree. He became a Tory M.P. in 1833 and was four times Prime Minister between 1868 and 1894.

No. 62 Rodney Street

No. 54 Rodney Street was the home of **Dr. W. H. Duncan (1805-1863),** Liverpool's first Medical Officer of Health from 1847 to 1863. This post was the first of its kind in the world. The appalling housing conditions of the 19th century in Liverpool, the rapidly increasing population and the cholera and typhoid epidemics in the town, obviously made such an appointment essential.

No. 35 Rodney Street was probably the first house built in the street. It was erected c. 1783-1784 on a site leased by William Roscoe.

HENRY BOOTH; NICHOLAS MONSARRAT; LIVERPOOL'S 'HARLEY STREET'.

Henry Booth (1789-1869), was born at **No. 34 Rodney Street.** He was a corn merchant and a founder and director of the Liverpool and Manchester Railway Company. A statue of him stands in the North Hall of St George's Hall holding the railway coupling which he invented.

No. 34 Rodney Street

North of Hardman Street is **No. 11 Rodney Street,** the birthplace of **Nicholas Monsarrat (1910-1979).** The son of a distinguished Liverpool surgeon, he wrote the best seller *'The Cruel Sea'* in 1951. It described his experiences in a Corvette in the North Atlantic as part of the Liverpool Escort Force during the Second World War. The Corvette berthed in Albert Dock during the air raids of 1941. Nicholas Monsarrat was buried at sea as was his wish.

* City of Liverpool Wall Plaque

0   ¼ Km   ¼ mile

Scale

The sites of **Bold Street,** together with **Renshaw Street** and a number of other streets in this area, were originally rope walks in elongated yards to facilitate spinning. This was an important industry for Liverpool well into the 19th century when sailing ships still reigned supreme. Nelson's H.M.S. *'Victory'* had 32 kilometres (20 miles) of rope in its rigging, which gives an indication of the demand for rope.

Sebastian Ziani de Ferranti (1864-1930) was born at this end of Bold Street. An electrical engineer and inventor, he took out 176 patents during his lifetime. When in Deptford, London in his early twenties, he planned an electrical supply system that served large areas of London north of the Thames. The principles embodied in the system are now standard practice throughout the world.

HENRY BERRY; DUKE STREET; SCANDINAVIAN HOTEL; GLADYS AYLWARD.

Berry Street is named after **Henry Berry (1728-1812),** Liverpool's second dock engineer. He was the engineer for the Sankey Canal which was opened in 1757 and runs from the River Mersey to St Helens. It is claimed that the canal was Britain's first true industrial canal, in that its channel was totally independent of the Sankey Brook which it paralled. Mr Berry lived in a house originally on the east corner of Berry Street and Upper Duke Street.

Duke Street is named after the **Duke of Cumberland,** King George II's brother. He honoured Liverpool by a Royal Inspection in appreciation of the town's support for his brother when the Scots rebelled in 1745.

The **former Congregational Church,** now the Blackie Arts Centre, has an unusual stone drum and domed roof. It was built in 1840-41 and designed by **Joseph Franklin (c. 1785-1855).**

Former Congregational Church

The stucco building, on the corner of Duke Street and Nelson Street, was formerly the **Scandinavian Hotel.** It housed many of the Scandinavians who passed through the town in the 19th century either as emigrants or seamen. This area provided many boarding houses for **Swedes, Norwegian, Germans** and **Spaniards** who arrived as members of ships' crews. 40 per cent of able seamen who signed on in sailing ships in 1891 were foreigners!

Rodney Street has long been known as Liverpool's *'Harley Street',* because of the surgeries and consulting rooms of doctors and specialists. **Dr Ambrose Dawson** was the first doctor to move into the street in 1790, when it was still being developed.

The medical profession has made a distinguished contribution to Liverpool's heritage over the years. **Dr Matthew Dobson,** who died in 1784, was a physician to the Liverpool Infirmary. His work on diabetes is recognised as one of the three steps which eventually led to its control. **Dr James Currie (1756-1805),** a Liverpool **Scot,** was an acknowledged authority on Robert Burns and was his first biographer.

ST LUKE'S CHURCH; ROPE WALKS; SEBASTIAN ZIANI DE FERRANTI.

St Luke's Church was originally designed in 1802 by **John Foster senior.** The design was reworked by his son **John Foster junior** and completed in 1831. It is notable for the large number of male and female heads covering the building. How many heads of each sex are there? The church suffered war damage in 1941 and it was purchased, with its gardens, by the City Council as a place of rest and tranquility after the war.

No. 20 Nelson Street was selected by **Gladys Aylward (1902-1970)** to become a Chinese Gospel Mission in 1953. Miss Aylward returned to England from China in 1948.

Gladys Aylward was a parlour maid before her firm Christian beliefs took her to China. With only £5 on her person, and no knowledge of any Chinese dialect, she was nevertheless determined to win converts in that vast country. Her life story was portrayed by **Ingrid Bergman** in the film *'The Inn of the Sixth Happiness'.* The film was shot in North Wales and the cast included many Liverpool Chinese children.

'CHINA TOWN'; KWOK FONG; HUGH OWEN THOMAS; SIR ROBERT JONES; KITTY WILKINSON.

This area is identified with the Chinese community, which is the oldest established in Europe. Ships had picked up Chinese seamen in ones and twos as replacement crews long before the middle of the 19th century, but the Chinese were not seen in any numbers until Alfred Holt began recruiting Chinese seamen in 1892-1893. The Chinese population could be counted in a few hundreds in 1906, but had probably doubled by 1939.

'Chinatown' has many shops, restaurants and facilities run by the Chinese community. These include the Chinese pub named *'The Nook'* in Nelson Street. One of the most famous characters of the area was **Kwok Fong (1882-1969).** He spent his boyhood a few miles from Canton, and as a pigtailed youth, made his way to Hong Kong where he went to sea in a Liverpool ship. After several voyages to the Mersey, he decided to settle in Liverpool near the river in the early 1900s.

Kwok Fong visited ships with Chinese crews, and sold necessities to the seamen, who did not wish to venture ashore in an alien city. His main work, however, which continued for 50 years, was the welfare of Asian crews who sailed under the flag of Liverpool shipping lines. The man, who was Mr Kwok to many Liverpudlians, was Uncle Fong of Liverpool to the scores of Chinese he befriended and helped over the years. He died aged 87 in Seel Street.

No. 11 Nelson Street, which is now an orthopaedic factory, housed the medical practice of **Hugh Owen Thomas** who was born in 1834 in Liverpool. He would attack his patients in order to snap their limbs back into position. He was despised by the medical establishment in Liverpool, but is known as the father of orthopaedics. He published, at his own expense, *'Knee, Hip and Ankle',* which in America was regarded as a pioneering masterpiece. Sadly in Britain he remained largely ignored.

His nephew, who later became **Sir Robert Jones (1857-1933),** took over the practice and further developed most of his uncle's techniques to great effect. He produced the first ever British x-rays in Nelson Street in 1895.

In **Upper Frederick Street** Liverpool Town Council set up Britain's first public wash-house in 1842 and **Kitty Wilkinson (1786-1860)** became its superintendent. Kitty Wilkinson was born in Londonderry and was from a humble background. She sacrificed her own happiness at an early age to care for her blind and mentally sick mother. She came to Liverpool and soon started a night school for neighbours' children during a cholera epidemic. During the 1832 epidemic, and without any public help, she prepared food for the hungry, nursed the sick and used her boiler to disinfect and wash the fever-tainted clothing of her neighbours. For such efforts, the Town Council established the wash-house.

Women have made an important contribution in Liverpool towards improving the lot of the poor, and this walk describes projects they undertook in various parts of the city centre. Other women instigated policies which improved services city wide. **Elizabeth Margaret (Bessie) Braddock (1899-1970),** was occupied from her early childhood with the social service and housing work begun by her mother **Mary Bamber.** Bessie Braddock was a member of the Liverpool City Council from 1930 till 1961, and became an M.P. in 1945. Her strong views on the housing needs of Liverpool people were frequently expressed in the House of Commons.

DUKES TERRACE; THE ROYAL INSTITUTION; NATHANIEL HAWTHORNE.

Nos. 159-175 Duke Street, of which only two remain, were originally merchants houses built in 1765. In the 19th century the merchants gradually moved further out, selling these houses separately from the gardens behind which were then built on. Here a *'back to back'* terrace for artisans was built and named **Dukes Terrace.** Access was obtained by means of an alley under the frontage properties. Dukes Terrace is the last surviving example of *'back to back'* housing in the city centre, and the dwellings were occupied until the early 1970s. Working class housing in the first part of the 19th century was often built around courts. Two communal 'privies' or earth closets per court and one cold tap were usually the only sanitary provision. The City's Medical Officer of Health said in 1882 that, *'Whole districts are as plagued as the cholera smitten cities of India'.*

The **Royal Institution** in Colquitt Street was originally built in about 1799 as a house for **Thomas Parr,** an important Liverpool banker. Mr. Parr boasted that he had – *'The handsomest house, wife and horse in Liverpool'.* In 1817 the building was taken over to house the future **Royal Institution,** an organisation established in the early 19th century for the cultivation of literature, science and the arts. It was incorporated by Royal Charter in 1822. The building was until recently owned by Liverpool University as a centre for further education. For administrative reasons, the building was closed in the 1980s and sold.

Kitty Wilkinson

Royal Institution

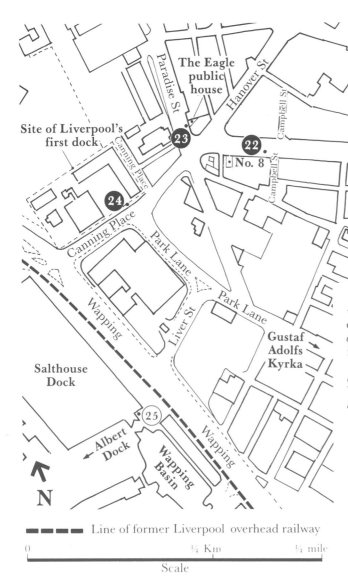

Line of former Liverpool overhead railway

Scale

0   ¼ Km   ¼ mile

The building has played an important role in Liverpool's cultural life for nearly 200 years and many famous people have passed through its portals. **John James Audubon (c 1780-1851)** the **American** artist, arrived in Liverpool in 1836 with over 400 illustrations of birds. Liverpool Society supported him and he held a very successful exhibition at the Royal Institution.

To the west of the Royal Institution, on Seel Street, is the oldest remaining Roman Catholic Church in Liverpool. Dated 1788, it is now the **Polish Roman Catholic Church of St Peter in Liverpool.**

No. 153 Duke Street was, in the 19th century, **Mrs Blodgett's boarding house.** This establishment was popular with the **American** captains of emigrant ships. **Nathaniel Hawthorne (1804-1864),** the **American** author and U.S. Consul in Liverpool, lodged here in 1856 to 1857. One of America's foremost writers, and author of *'Tanglewood Tales'* and *'Scarlet Letter',* he remarked that the English climate was the best thing we had, and the only thing we did not brag about.

FELICIA HEMANS; COLONEL BOLTON; JOHN BELLINGHAM; LIVERPOOL CLOCKMAKERS.

No. 118 Duke Street was the birthplace of the poet, **Felicia Dorothea Hemans, née Browne (1793-1835).** Her first volume of poems was written between the age of eight and 13, and she went on to write many works to earn her living. She attracted an enormous **American** following for her poem, *'The Landing of the Pilgrim Fathers',* which was traditionally recited in the family circle at Thanksgiving. Her best known work, *'Casabianca',* commences with the famous line *'The boy stood on the burning deck . . .'* On her death, no less a figure than **William Wordsworth** described her as *'That Holy Spirit, Sweet as the Spring, as Ocean deep'.*

Felicia Hemans

In 1789 **Colonel Bolton** took up residence at **No. 116 Duke Street.** A staunch patriot, in 1803 he equipped a regiment of 600 volunteers at his own expense. In 1805, he shot down a subordinate officer in an enforced duel. At the inquest Colonel Bolton was found guilty of murder but was never charged as public opinion was behind him. The duel was the last to take place in Liverpool.

Nos. 107-125 Duke Street is a multi-storey garage, but has previously been a terrace of houses. **John Bellingham (1771-1812)** took up residence in one of them in the early 19th century. He was the only man ever to assassinate a British prime minister. A native of St Neots, he was a timber contractor who went to Russia to further his business. Whilst there he was arrested for debt and thrown into jail. His application to the British Ambassador for help was refused, and on his release he returned to Britain and Duke Street.

He campaigned for redress from the British Government for the injustice he claimed he received from the Russians, but to no avail, and this lack of interest rankled. In May 1812 he went to London where he purchased two pistols. He shot **Prime Minister Spencer Perceval** dead in the Lobby of the House of Commons. Within a week of committing the crime he was tried, convicted, sentenced and executed. Ironically, the next Prime Minister was the **Earl of Liverpool.**

No. 105 Duke Street was built as the **Union News Room.** It was opened on 1st January 1801, the day England was united with Ireland. It was designed by **John Foster senior.**

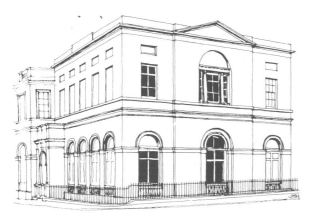

Former Union News Room

Nos. 30-32 Slater Street with their long horizontal bands of windows are late 18th century buildings associated with watch and clock making. Prescot and Liverpool were important centres for clock making between the 17th and early 19th centuries. Famous clockmakers include **Aspinwall, Wyke, Wycherley, Finney, Scotson, Herdman, Roskell, Walton, Litherland** and **Tobias.**

FAWCETT PRESTON'S; SARAH BIFFIN.

Just south of here formerly stood the works of **Fawcett Preston,** known locally as *'Fossets'.* It was founded in 1758 by **George Perry,** a **Scot,** to make household utensils. Perry was succeeded by a **Mr Fawcett,** who manufactured guns for Wellington's army. The guns were also used at the Mexican War of 1842, and by both sides in the U.S. Civil War. The first shot of the Civil War was fired from a *'Fosset's'* gun.

No. 8 Duke Street was originally a house which stood on part of the site of the present commercial building. The house was the last known home of **Sarah Biffin (1784-1850).** Sarah Biffin was only one metre (39″) in height, and without arms. She spent most of her life as a fairground exhibit. However, her fame rests on her abilities as a miniature portrait painter, having learned to paint with the end of the handle fixed to a loop on her right shoulder, and manipulating the brush with her mouth. She was patronised by King George III, George IV, William IV and Queen Victoria and her work was hung in the Royal Academy. She died at No. 8 Duke Street.

Sarah Biffin

PARADISE STREET; JAMES MAURY; THE EAGLE PUBLIC HOUSE.

Paradise Street was originally on the line of the **Pool of Liverpool.** This stretched from the river, to what is now the main entrance to the first Mersey road tunnel at Old Haymarket. After the construction of Liverpool's first dock in the early 18th century at the mouth of the Pool, the Pool was culverted underground and Paradise Street formed. The culvert was the work of **Thomas Steers,** who designed Liverpool's first dock.

The area was very colourful, particularly in the early 19th century. Paradise Street was a street of ill repute, and brothels and grog shops were prevalent. **James Maury, America's** first ever Consul, had his office here. One of his duties was to arrange the release of **American** sailors from gaol due to waterfront brawls. At this time, there were nearly 2,300 drinking dens in the city centre, many of which were located in this area.

Paradise Street was known across the oceans of the world and is immortalised in the sea shanty:

'Now as I was a walking down Paradise Street,
Hey-ho blow the man down . . .
. . . Blow him away to Liverpool Town'.

There was no shortage of houses where *'Seamen's lodging house'* could be seen scrawled over the door. Here, exorbitant charges would be demanded for a sailor to be fed and bedded in some sort of fashion. **Charles Dickens,** on one of his many visits to Liverpool, had much sympathy for the Liverpool seaman and commented – *'Poor Mercantile Jack – ill lodged, ill fed, ill used, hocussed, entrapped, anticipated, cleaned out'.*

Charles Dickens

The **Eagle public house,** on the east side of Paradise Street, has had many uses during the building's history, including a pawnshop, coffee rooms, a boarding house and a beer house. 100 years ago it was named the *'American Eagle',* and no doubt emigrants stayed here when waiting for their ships to depart.

THOMAS STEERS AND LIVERPOOL'S FIRST DOCK; GUSTAF ADOLFS KYRKA.

The modern commercial development adjacent to this marker is built on one of the most historically important sites in Liverpool.

At the beginning of the 18th century, this site was the mouth of the **Pool of Liverpool** where it joined the River Mersey. In 1708, **Thomas Steers** was appointed to advise on the building of the town's first dock. He proposed that

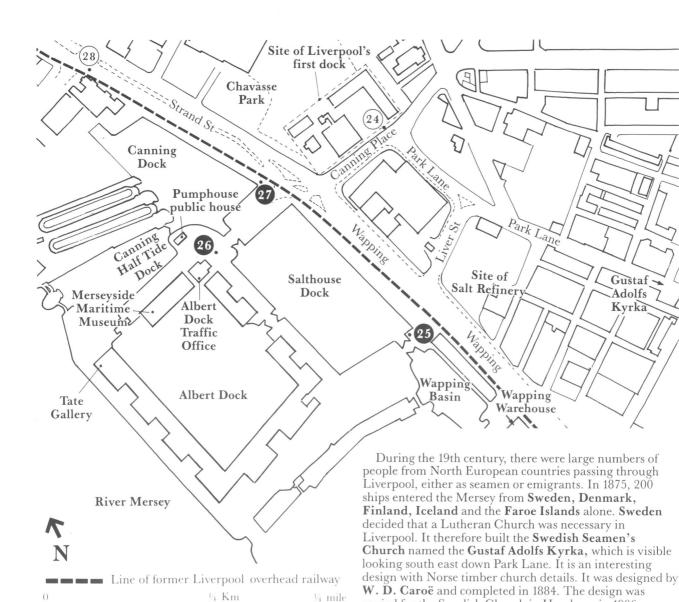

Site of Liverpool's first dock

Chavasse Park

Strand St

Canning Dock

Pumphouse public house

Canning Half Tide Dock

Merseyside Maritime Museum

Albert Dock Traffic Office

Tate Gallery

Albert Dock

River Mersey

Salthouse Dock

Canning Place

Park Lane

Wapping

Liver St

Park Lane

Site of Salt Refinery

Gustaf Adolfs Kyrka

Wapping

Wapping Basin

Wapping Warehouse

N

▬ ▬ ▬ Line of former Liverpool overhead railway

0   ¼ Km   ¼ mile

Scale

During the 19th century, there were large numbers of people from North European countries passing through Liverpool, either as seamen or emigrants. In 1875, 200 ships entered the Mersey from **Sweden, Denmark, Finland, Iceland** and the **Faroe Islands** alone. **Sweden** decided that a Lutheran Church was necessary in Liverpool. It therefore built the **Swedish Seamen's Church** named the **Gustaf Adolfs Kyrka,** which is visible looking south east down Park Lane. It is an interesting design with Norse timber church details. It was designed by **W. D. Caroë** and completed in 1884. The design was copied for the Swedish Church in Hamburg in 1906.

Thomas Steers

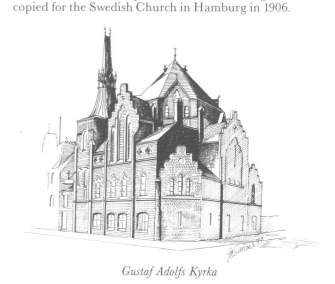

Gustaf Adolfs Kyrka

the mouth of the Pool be converted to a dock controlled by flood gates, and Liverpool's first dock was opened in 1715. Although the idea of floodgates was not new, their use to enclose a harbour was an innovation subsequently followed the world over.

Thomas Steers was of Dutch origin, but came to Liverpool from London. He was also the engineer for other docks in Liverpool and he built piers, canals, Liverpool's first water supply system and a theatre. He also designed the now demolished St George's Church in Derby Square, and to top it all became the Mayor of Liverpool in 1739-1740!

25
LIVERPOOL HERITAGE WALK

SALTHOUSE DOCK; SALT REFINING; WAPPING WAREHOUSE; THE PRESS GANG.

The present **Salthouse Dock,** immediately north of this marker between Albert Dock and the dock road, was reconstructed and enlarged in 1845, on the site of earlier docks which dated from 1753.

In 1611 crude brine salt was manufactured in Liverpool, and in 1696 the first proper refinery works was built to process salt from Northwich in Cheshire. The refinery was founded by **John Blackburne,** and Salthouse Dock takes its name from the works which were originally located due east of this point.

Wapping Warehouse is visible just south of **Wapping Basin.** It was constructed between 1851 and 1856 to provide secure storage for general cargoes to designs by **Jesse Hartley,** who had earlier designed Albert Dock Warehouses. Extensive restoration of the building was undertaken between 1986 and 1988 by the Merseyside Development Corporation, prior to the building's conversion into flats.

In the late 18th and early 19th centuries there was a **Press Gang Office** located near this point. Seamen from both this country and abroad, were coerced into joining the Royal Navy, particularly during the Napoleonic Wars. No sooner was the Press Gang seen on the streets than the public warning cry went up, *'Hawks abroad'.*

ALBERT DOCK; JESSE HARTLEY; ALBERT DOCK TRAFFIC OFFICE; PUMPHOUSE PUBLIC HOUSE; CAPTAIN MATTHEW WEBB; JOHN MASEFIELD

Albert Dock was built between 1841 and 1848. It was opened by **Prince Albert** in July 1846 when he attended a great banquet in the building. The whole complex, with the exception of the Dock Traffic Office, was designed by Jesse Hartley and cost £514,475, a vast sum in those days. It comprises a series of perimeter blocks, each of five storeys and a basement. No wood is used in the construction, other than for piling, making it completely fire proof.

It is one of the earliest enclosed docks in the world, and a complete example of the type. The enclosed water area covers three hectares (7½ acres), and the warehouses contain 120,000 sq metres (1.3 million sq ft) of floorspace. It is the greatest monument to Jesse Hartley, the dock engineer of the time.

Jesse Hartley (1780-1860), a Yorkshireman, was born in Pontefract. He was trained as a stonemason and became Bridgemaster to the West Riding. He was appointed Liverpool Dock Engineer in 1824. **Sir James Picton,** the Liverpool architect and historian, described him as: *'Of large build and powerful frame, rough in humour and occasionally even rude, using expletives which the angel of mercy would not like to record.'*

Jesse Hartley

Albert Dock was used as a bonded warehouse until after the Second World War, and rum was stored in its basement and tobacco on the upper floors. In the early 1980s the dock was dredged and refilled with water and the buildings were restored by the Merseyside Development Corporation. New uses for the buildings include shops, offices, the Merseyside Maritime Museum and the Tate Gallery.

The **Albert Dock Traffic Office** was completed in 1847 and designed by **Philip Hardwick (1792-1870).** The columns, like those round Albert Dock, are of hollow cast iron. The portico above is also of cast iron. It is now used by Granada TV as a news centre.

The **Pumphouse public house** was formerly an hydraulic power building. Steam driven pumps pressurised water, which was then conveyed through pipes to operate lock gates, cranes and hoists within the adjacent dock area. Many of the hydraulic power hoists remain at Albert Dock, although they are no longer in use.

The **Tate Gallery,** occupying part of Albert Dock near the river, is a sister gallery to the Tate in London. The London gallery was made a gift to the nation by **Henry Tate** of Tate & Lyle. He originally started the famous sugar business in Liverpool.

Albert Dock

Outside the **Merseyside Maritime Museum** is a large anchor originally belonging to H.M.S. *'Nile'.* It was later converted into the H.M.S. *'Conway'* training ship based on the Mersey. **Captain Matthew Webb (1848-1883)** who was the first person to swim the English Channel served on H.M.S. *'Conway'* as a cadet. He lost his life attempting to swim the rapids below Niagara Falls. **John Masefield (1878-1967),** the Poet Laureate, also came to Liverpool, and served as a cadet on H.M.S. *'Conway'.* Illness prevented him from following a life at sea but he wrote many poems about it, including *'Sea Fever'* – *'I must go down to the seas again, to the lonely sea and the sky'.* He wrote more poems to commemorate events on Merseyside than any other poet.

MOUTH OF THE POOL; GEORGE CANNING; LIVERPOOL OVERHEAD RAILWAY; CAPTAIN NOEL CHAVASSE, V.C.

This point is on the original shoreline of the Mersey, hence the name of the dock road here – **Strand Street,** meaning *'Shore Street'.* It is also the point at which the mouth of the Pool joined the Mersey and, after 1715, the point where Liverpool's first dock was connected to the river.

With the exception of the first dock and Stanley Dock north of the city centre which were both located inland, all the other Liverpool docks were created on the river side of

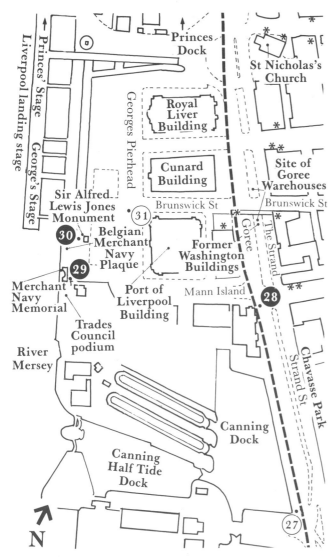

Overhead Railway Poster

Line of former Liverpool overhead railway

* City of Liverpool Wall Plaque

0   ¼ Km   ¼ mile

Scale

the Mersey's natural banks. This was achieved by extending encircling quays to enclose dock basins.

Chadwick's Map of 1725 shows a pier at this point stretching into the river, probably to allow sailing ships to wait for the wind. By 1737 the first dock was overloaded and so a new basin was constructed to form a larger outer harbour. This was reconstructed in 1813 and named **Canning Dock,** which is the present basin due north of this point. It was named after **George Canning (1770-1827),** who was M.P. for Liverpool from 1812 to 1823. He became Prime Minister in 1827 but sadly died the same year.

Herman Melville (1819-1891), the **American** author, in Liverpool on his first seafaring voyage in 1839, marvelled at Liverpool's docks and compared them with the Great Wall of China and the Pyramids of the Pharoahs. At the height of their activity there was a total of 57 kilometres (35½ miles) of quays on both sides of the river.

The **Liverpool overhead railway** ran alongside Canning Dock on gantries 4.8 metres (16') high. It was opened in 1895 and operated until 1956. It ran 12 kilometres (7½ miles) from Seaforth Sands in the north to Dingle in the south and had 17 stations. It was the first electric overhead railway in the world and its construction was necessary as the dock road was so congested. It afforded splendid views of the busy docks and being used mainly by dockers it became known as the *'Dockers umbrella'.*

Across Strand Street to the east is **Chavasse Park,** named after **Captain Noel Chavasse, V.C. (1884-1917),** the son of Bishop Chavasse, the principal founder of Liverpool Cathedral. Captain Chavasse, an old boy of Liverpool College, was a former Olympic athlete and a Medical Officer in the 10th Battalion, Liverpool Scottish Regiment in the First World War. He won the Victoria Cross twice. He also obtained the Military Cross. Sadly he died in Belgium from war wounds in 1917.

GORÉE PIAZZAS; THE SLAVE TRADE; WASHINGTON IRVING; NATHANIEL HAWTHORNE.

Looking north from this spot is a wide dual carriageway flanked by large buildings on each side. This carriageway originally contained warehouses and the overhead railway, hence its present great width. The western carriageway is known as **Gorée,** and the eastern one as **The Strand.** The former takes its name from the African island off Cape Verde. It ran parallel to the Gorée Warehouses, known as **Gorée Piazzas,** which were rebuilt in 1802 after a disastrous fire and finally demolished after air raid damage in 1941. The ground floor contained an open arcade and legend has it that slaves were sold here, tethered to bulky iron rings attached to the walls.

Liverpool's wealth was based on a system of trade comprising two triangles of commerce within which slavery formed an integral part. Broadly, the trading pattern involved a first route built up after 1700 along which ships carried cotton goods and hardware items to West Africa and from there, slaves and ivory to the West Indies, returning home loaded with sugar, rum and tobacco. The other route, partly followed by those who abhorred slavery, took salt to the North American Coast; coal and salt fish from there down to the West Indies returning home with sugar, rum, tobacco and molasses.

The *'Liverpool Merchant'* is the first recorded Liverpool slaver – she sold her cargo of 220 Africans at Barbados in the 1740s. The last legal slaving voyage was made by

Captain Hugh *'Mind Your Eye'* Crow of Liverpool in July 1807 in *'Kitty's Amelia'*. Slavery was abolished in England in 1776 as the result of the Mansfield Judgement in the High Court and the British slave trade overseas was terminated by Act of Parliament in 1807. To their shame, Liverpool Corporation and the town's merchants in African trade fiercely resisted abolition and 64 petitions were submitted to both House of Parliament, but to no avail. There was, however, also a lobby of certain prominent Liverpudlians who campaigned for aboliton of *'the horrid trade'*, prominent among them the Rathbone family and William Roscoe.

The Black population of Liverpool is one of the oldest established in the country, dating from the 18th and early 19th centuries. The early residents were mainly either the servants of wealthy families with connections in the West Indies, or seamen recruited as replacements for dead or diseased European sailors from the West Indies, West Africa or the United States.

Washington Irving (1783-1859), the **American** author, managed his brother's business at **No. 1 Gorée Warehouses** from 1815 to 1818. When the business failed, Irving had a nervous breakdown and whilst convalescing with relatives in Birmingham, England recalled his childhood and wrote the famous *'Rip Van Winkle'* story.

The Gorée Piazzas consisted of two blocks running north to south. **Washington Buildings** occupied the northern end of the southern block adjacent to Brunswick Street. **Nathaniel Hawthorne (1804-1864),** the author and **American** Consul in Liverpool, had his office in this building from 1853 to 1857.

The corner of Mann Island and Strand Street between 1895 and 1956 was the site of four rail transportation systems. Below ground was, and still is, the Mersey underground railway to the Wirral. At ground level the dock goods railway and Liverpool Corporation tram tracks crossed each other, and on supports in the air was the overhead railway.

PIER HEAD; RIVER MERSEY; MERSEY FERRIES; MERCHANT NAVY MEMORIAL; LIVERPOOL TRADES COUNCIL PODIUM.

The **Pier Head** takes its name from a stone pier built in the 1760s. It was known as the North Pier, and stretched out into the Mersey. It projected from the then quay adjacent to St Nicholas's Church just north of the Royal Liver Building. It is still visible on maps published prior to 1810, after which it was integrated into quay works associated with the construction of Princes Dock which opened in 1821. The Pier Head has been called the, *'Threshold to the ends of the Earth'*.

The earliest mention of the **River Mersey** is in a deed from the reign of **Ethelred II, A.D. 1004.** The name derives from the Old English Maere, meaning boundary, and has a connection with the name of the Kingdom of Mercia of which the river formed a northern boundary.

It is not know when the **first ferry** crossed the Mersey, but it is generally agreed that it could have been in 1207, when Liverpool received its charter from **King John.** The passage across the Mersey was undertaken by the borough, which charged a toll. However, it was at Birkenhead that the ferry services were to be established on a permanent and regular basis. In 1150 **Hamo de Mascy, third Baron of Dunham,** granted land for a Benedictine Priory at Birkenhead. In 1330, **King Edward III** granted the Benedictine monks the legal right to ferry to Liverpool.

The **Merchant Navy memorial** in Portland stone by the river was built to commemorate the 1,390 officers and men who died whilst serving with the Royal Navy during the Second World War and have no grave but the sea. It is a national memorial maintained by the Commonwealth War Graves Commission. The sculpture in the memorial incorporating terrestrial and celestial globes is by **H. Tyson Smith,** the Liverpool sculptor.

The **steel podium** just south of the memorial was erected by the **Liverpool Trades Council** during its 125th anniversary celebrations. On it is a plaque by Liverpool sculptor, Arthur Dooley, illustrating the *'Unity of European Labour'*.

Near to this area once fronting Mann Island, stood a public house known as *'Dicky Sam's'*. This name was probably derived from the licensee **Richard Samuel,** who kept it at one time. Liverpool sailors were once known as *'Dicky Sams'* all over the world due to the fame of the inn.

PORT OF LIVERPOOL BUILDING; SIR ALFRED LEWIS JONES; BELGIAN MERCHANT NAVY PLAQUE; LIVERPOOL LANDING STAGE; EARLY STEAMSHIPS.

The southernmost building of the Pier Head trio is the **Port of Liverpool Building.** Designed by **Arnold Thornely** and completed in 1907 it is built in Portland stone. The building could be said to utilise the dome of St. Paul's Cathedral rising above the centre of a renaissance palace. The great majority of the docks system in the Mersey estuary is administered from this building.

Port of Liverpool Building   S. Long

Near the river bank stands the monument to **Sir Alfred Lewis Jones (1845-1909).** It was erected in 1913 and the sculptor was **Sir George Frampton.** Below the crowned female figure is a panel depicting Sir Alfred above allegorical figures at the base. Sir Alfred as a young man joined the administrative staff of the Elder Dempster Line, which shipped fruit into Liverpool from West Africa. He promoted the eating of bananas which were then an almost unknown fruit in Britain. He also introduced refrigeration into ships and was the founder of the Liverpool School of Tropical Medicine, the world's first, which opened in 1898. This school discovered that mosquito bites are the cause of malaria.

Adjacent to Sir Alfred's memorial is an upstand wall which incorporates **a plaque** dedicated to **831 seamen of the Belgian navy who died at sea during the Second World War.** It was erected by the Federation of Belgian Merchant Seamen.

The **floating Liverpool landing stage** is visible a short distance from the river bank. The present landing stage dates only from the mid 1970s and is about half the length of the previous one, which dated from the 1870s and was the largest floating structure in the world at the time. It was one kilometre (0.6 miles) in length. The former and present landing stages, although a single structure, are divided into two parts by name – the **George's Stage** in front of the

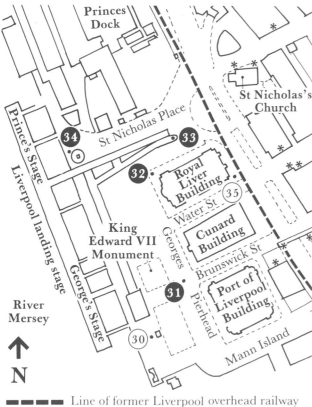

Line of former Liverpool overhead railway

✱ City of Liverpool Wall Plaque

Scale

Pier Head buildings and the **Princes Stage** a little further north. The George's Stage is used by the various cross river ferries with the Princes Stage serving the sea and ocean-going ships.

Standing by the river, the early steamships that crossed the Atlantic to and from Liverpool can be recalled. The first was the *'Savannah',* which in 1819 made the first steam crossing. It left Savannah, Georgia on 22nd May arriving in Liverpool on 20th June. It had sails as well as steam power and had to rely on the sails for 90% of the voyage time.

In 1838 Liverpool built the paddle steamer *'Royal William'* – the first steamship to make the west bound crossing to New York, a trip which took 15 days. A few months later the Liverpool built ship *'Liverpool'* became the first two-funnelled steamer to cross the Atlantic. This ship initiated the transatlantic service. In 1845 Isambard Kingdom Brunel's *'Great Britain'* set off from Liverpool on its maiden voyage to New York. This was the first iron steamer which used a screw propeller.

MONUMENT TO KING EDWARD VII; THE CUNARD BUILDING; SAMUEL CUNARD; CUNARD SHIPS.

From this point the former **Bank of England** building is visible up Brunswick Street. In the days when the Mersey was full of shipping and congestion was quite common, ships would come up the Mersey and anchor in mid river once the Bank of England came into view, tying up when space became available.

The **equestrian monument to King Edward VII** was unveiled in 1921 and is by **Sir W. Goscombe John.** There are four regal equestrian statues in Liverpool – this one at the Pier Head, Queen Victoria and Prince Albert at St George's Plateau, and King George III at Monument Place

in London Road. Liverpool is unusual in possessing so many, as there are only 26 equestrian statues of royalty in Britain as a whole.

The **Cunard Building** was originally the headquarters of the Cunard Steamship Company. It was designed by **Willink and Thicknesse** of Liverpool and completed in 1916. It is built of Portland stone and is in the style of an

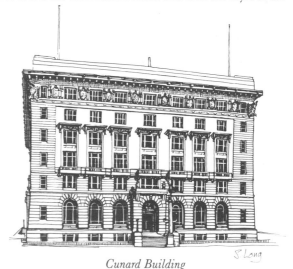

Cunard Building

Italian palazzo. The eagles on the corners of the building, supporting the shields of the Cunard Company, were each carved from a single block of stone weighing 45.5 tonnes (43 tons). It was in the boardroom of this building that the decision was taken to build the gigantic Queen Mary and Queen Elizabeth liners, which were Liverpool registered ships.

Samuel Cunard was born in Nova Scotia, Canada in 1787. He came to Liverpol in 1840 to start the firm's liner service between Liverpool, Halifax and Boston. He had put in a successful tender to win the British Admiralty's contract to carry mail by steamship between England and North America, and Cunard's was the first steamship to introduce a regular transatlantic mail service.

Samuel Cunard

The first ship, the *'Britannia',* was a paddle steamer which left Liverpool on 4th July, 1840 – America's Independence Day – with mails and passengers for Canada and America. The Company owned many famous ships, including the *'Lusitania'* and the *'Mauretania',* – all the ships' names generally ending in *'ia'.*

Steamships ultimately cut the travelling time from Liverpool to North America from 28 to 3½ days, and the Cunard ships were noted for speed. In 1919 Cunard's express service to New York was transferred to Southampton. The Cunard Company and the White Star Line, also a Liverpool company, were amalgamated in 1934. The last Cunard liner left Liverpool in 1966 after 126 years of association with the port.

ROYAL LIVER BUILDING;
LIVER BIRD.

The Royal Liver Friendly Society was formed in 1850 as a burial club by nine Liverpool workers. Five years later it had agents in most towns in Britain and it is now one of the largest companies of its type in Britain. The **Royal Liver Building** is its headquarters; opened in 1911, it was designed by **W. Aubrey Thomas (c 1859-1939)**. It is faced in granite and is one of the world's first multi-storey buildings to have a reinforced concrete structure. The two sculptured clock towers are surmounted by domes on which

Royal Liver Building

the famous mythical Liver Birds are perched. They are made of copper and are 5.5m (18') high. The clock faces are 7.6m (25') in diameter, making them the largest public striking clocks in Britain.

The origin of the **Liver Bird** is as follows:
King John, in 1207, requiring a port for the conquest of Ireland, granted letters patent to Liverpool and the town adopted a corporate seal – the eagle of St John, the emblem of the House of King John. During the siege of 1644, when cavalier forces sacked Liverpool, the seal was lost. In 1655 it was replaced by a second seal but this did not resemble an eagle, possibly due to the ignorance or artistic shortcomings of the designer. As time went by the bird, which looked like a seagull, came to be regarded as a cormorant as such birds are prevalent in the Mersey. In the bird's beak is a sprig of foliage, probably of broom, the *'planta genista'* symbol of the Plantagenets.

Liver Bird

COLONEL H. R. DUFFIE, PORT
COMMANDER, U.S. ARMY;
AMERICAN G.I.'s; ELEANOR
ROOSEVELT; PRINCES DOCK

To the west is the former floating roadway which led down to the Princes and George's Landing Stages. In a small garden off the bus station is a **memorial stone** fixed to the southern wall of the floating roadway perimeter. It was given by **Colonel H. R. Duffie, Port Commander, U. S. Army,** and reads:

'Here in the dark days of war and in the dawn of victory, American troops and cargoes moved through this port furthered by British and Americans working together. This stone records their unity in accomplishing their mission. Erected by the 15th Port U.S.A. 1944.'

1,200,000 **American** G.I.s disembarked at Liverpool during the Second World War, prior to going to camps in various parts of Britain. Thousands of G.I.s were stationed in camps around Liverpool at Aintree, Haydock, Burtonwood and Sealand, and special trains brought them into Liverpool Central Station for entertainment in the evenings and at weekends. **Eleanor Roosevelt** visited Liverpool in November 1942 on a tour of U.S. Forces. Inside the enormous Stanley Warehouse in the North Docks she inspected U.S. stores, using a jeep as the floor areas were so large.

Throughout the war Liverpool handled a total of 76.2 million tonnes (75 million tons) of cargo mainly from the U.S. including 19.3 million tonnes (19 million tons) of imported **American** foodstuffs.

Princes Dock, to the north, was opened in 1821 and was designed by **John Foster and his son.** It was the first of the docks to be enclosed by walls, an arrangement which was subsequently employed throughout the dock system.

DEPARTURE POINT OF THE LINERS;
EMIGRATION; ACTIVITY IN THE
EARLY 20TH CENTURY; 'TITANIC
MEMORIAL'.

This area is one of the most important in Liverpool, as it was here that millions of people embarked and disembarked from the great ocean-going ships. It was an area which generated high emotion – the sadness of leaving Europe and relatives and friends, combined with the hopeful expectation of a better life across the oceans of the world. For many inward bound passengers it was their first sight of Europe.

Between 1830 and 1930 some nine million emigrants sailed from Liverpool for America. In 1852 the emigrant fare on an Inman Line ship was six guineas, but this plummetted for short periods to £2. 1907 was the year of the emigration peak, when Liverpool handled 177,000 people. They were mainly **British** and **Irish,** but also included large numbers of **Swedes, Norwegians** and **Russian Jews.**

The tourist and business trade was carried by the great liners of such companies as the Cunard, White Star and Canadian Pacific Lines. Samuel Cunard's ships started sailing in the 1840s, getting bigger through the 19th century. Airlines started taking passengers away from the liners from the 1930s onwards, as the speed and lower cost of air travel made travel by ship an increasing luxury. The last transatlantic liner left Liverpool for Canada in 1967.

Shipping activity in this area was at its height between 1895 and the early 1930s. At busy periods during this time the following scene could have occurred here:

At George's Landing Stage
– Eight ferries plying between the Pier Head and Egremont, New Brighton, Seacombe, Woodside (Birkenhead), Tranmere, Rock Ferry, New Ferry and

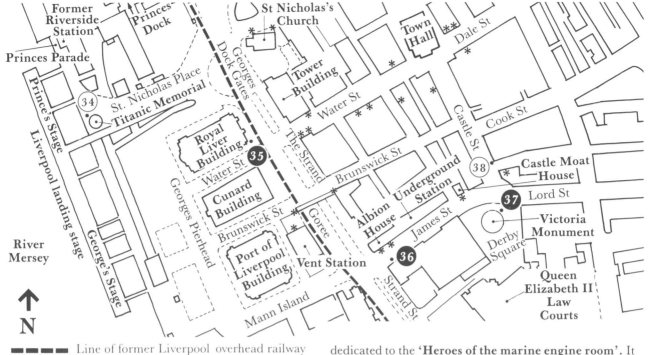

Eastham. Two luggage boats plying between the Pier Head and Birkenhead and Wallasey, carrying horses drawing carriages and carts as well as motor vehicles.

At Princes Landing Stage

– Two transatlantic liners, two Isle of Man ships, one Welsh boat sailing between Liverpool, Llandudno and the Menai Straits.

In Princes Dock

– One Dublin and one Belfast ferry boat.

At Riverside Station

– Two London boat trains bringing and taking passengers away.

In Princes Parade

– Large numbers of horses and carriages, horse drawn cabs and some private motor cars setting down and picking up passengers.

In the middle of this area the vertical stone monument cannot be missed. On Ordnance Survey maps it is entitled the **'Titanic Memorial'**. To avoid upsetting passengers boarding the liners, the monument itself was simply

dedicated to the **'Heroes of the marine engine room'**. It was paid for by international subscription, and was originally intended to commemorate the engineers and firemen lost in the Titanic disaster of 1912. The sculptor was **Sir W. Goscombe John,** and it was erected in 1916. Round the base are sculptural panels, the one facing St Nicholas's Church shows two stokers wearing *'Dicky Sam'* caps, which have long peaks to deflect the heat of the burning coals.

TOWER BUILDING; EARLS OF DERBY; FORMER GEORGE'S DOCK; VENTILATION STATION OF THE MERSEY ROAD TUNNEL.

Tower Building, to the east, was designed by **W. Aubrey Thomas (c. 1859-1934)** and was completed in 1908. It has glazed tiles to allow the dirt to be washed off by the rain and is one of the earliest steel framed buildings in the country.

Another building stood on this site in the 19th century and was the Liverpool end of a semaphore system stretching via Bidston Hill to Hilbre Island, and then via stations to Anglesey. This informed Liverpool of approaching ship movements.

Tower Building is on the site of the **Tower of Liverpool** fortified by **Sir John Stanley** in 1406. It was a fortified house on what was then the river's edge, belonging to the **Stanley family, Earls of Derby.** They used it as an embarkation base when visiting the Isle of Man and their

Prince's Landing Stage in the mid 1920's

26

Tower Building

properties in Ireland. Towards the end of the 18th century it fell into disrepair and became the town's gaol. At one time 4,000 **French** prisoners of war were incarcerated there, mainly captured by Liverpool privateers. It was demolished in 1819.

The **Earls of Derby's** principal residence is **Knowsley Hall** on the outskirts of Liverpool. Since the 12th century the Stanley family have been a decisive influence in English politics. They were appointed Lords Deputy in Ireland and *'Kings'* of Man in the 15th century. They favoured the Cavaliers in the Civil War and lost most of their lands. The Earl of the time lost his head. One Earl in 1822 became Prime Minister and several have been Mayors of Liverpool. They were known in recent times as the *'Kings of Lancashire'.*

The famous race at Epsom is called after the family. The *'Derby'* was first run at Wallasey over the Leasowes by a Lord Derby then in residence at Leasowe Castle.

Most of the present Pier Head group of buildings stand on the former **George's Dock**. The dock was opened in 1771 for new vessels requiring greater draught, particularly *'Man of War'* ships. The dock was originally served by a passage into Canning Dock which lies immediately to the south.

The **George's Dock Ventilation and Central Station of the Mersey Road Tunnel** (which must be the longest name for a building in Liverpool), was completed in 1934. The consultant architect was **Herbert J. Rowse (1887-1963),** who practised in Liverpool. It is a superb piece of 1930s architecture and is embellished with much sculpture by **Edward C. Thompson** and **George T. Capstick,** a partnership of two Liverpool sculptors. Above the main entrance door may be seen an image of the heroic days of motoring – a motorist wearing a strapped leather cap and goggles with a tyre below him.

Albion House

WHITE STAR LINE; 'TITANIC'; MERSEY UNDERGROUND RAILWAY; THE INVENTOR OF 'MECCANO.'

Albion House was formerly the White Star building and the headquarters of the Oceanic Steam Navigation Company (the White Star Line). The building was opened in 1898 and is by **Richard Norman Shaw** in association with the Liverpool architect **J. Francis Doyle.** It is of brick, with Portland Stone bands sometimes described as the *'streaky bacon'* style, and is very similar to Shaw's New Scotland Yard building adjacent to Big Ben in London.

T. H. Ismay founded the shipping line in 1869, and the company had many famous ships such as the *'Majestic', 'Olympic'* and *'Oceanic'* all ending in *'ic'.* The company's liners were renowned for their luxury and comfort and were a formidable rival to the Cunard liners. The most famous liner of all was the *'Titanic'* which hit an iceberg off Newfoundland on its maiden voyage in 1912. It went down sending nearly 1,500 people to a watery grave. The

R.M.S. "Titanic"

building was surrounded by an angry and anxious crowd in 1912 as news slowly began to filter through of the disaster. Friends and relatives of the crew and passengers demanded to know what had happened, and frightened White Star Line officials had to shout down the latest news from the balconies of the building.

Next door is **James Street underground railway station** which was opened in 1886. Now part of the Merseyrail system, it was originally part of the Mersey Railway running between Liverpool and the Wirral. Initially steam trains were used, and the atmosphere underground was so bad that the tunnel was nick-named *'The Sewer',* and the public reverted to cross river ferries. Its fortunes were turned round in 1903, however, when it was converted to electric traction and business boomed with the cleaner conditions.

Although no longer here, one of the properties in James Street, near to the station, was occupied early this century by Liverpool born **Frank Hornby (1863-1937)** who invented *'Meccano', 'Hornby Trains'* and *'Dinky Toys'.* This was his second factory prior to moving to larger premises in the suburbs of the city.

LIVERPOOL CASTLE; CIVIL WAR; VICTORIA MONUMENT; CASTLE MOAT HOUSE; EARLS OF SEFTON.

Derby Square was originally occupied by **Liverpool Castle.** This was built in 1235 on a peninsula formed by the Mersey to the west and the Pool of Liverpool to the east.

During the Civil War of 1642 to 1646 Liverpool was divided in its loyalties. **John Moore** led a group of townsmen who favoured the Roundhead cause. **Colonel Edward Norris** of Speke Hall, Governor of the Castle at the time, led the Royalists who at first held Liverpool Castle. In 1643 **Colonel Assheton** led a successful assault on the castle and John Moore became its governor.

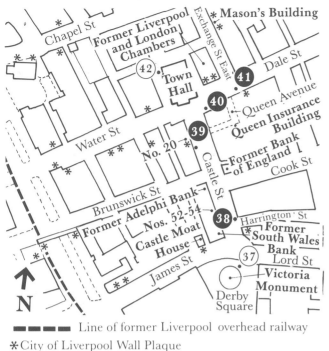

Line of former Liverpool overhead railway

* City of Liverpool Wall Plaque

Scale

Hill, Liverpool's shortest street, where **Daniel Defoe (1660-1731),** author of *'Robinson Crusoe',* stayed.

The **Molyneux family, Earls of Sefton,** were for many years *'Constables'* of the former Liverpool Castle. They lived at **Croxteth Hall** on the outskirts of Liverpool until the early 1970s, when the last Earl died and the line ceased. Horse racing started at Aintree in north Liverpool in 1829 and Lord Sefton introduced steeple chasing there in the 1840s. One of his races, the *'Grand National',* has been run at Aintree each year ever since.

38 CASTLE STREET; JOHN SADLER; BANK OF ENGLAND; FORMER ADELPHI BANK

During the 18th century **Castle Street** was known as the Fleet Street of Liverpool because of the many newspaper offices located in the area. Liverpool's first newspaper, Williamson's *'Liverpool Advertiser',* was first published in Castle Street on 25th May 1776.

Nos. 52-54 Castle Street, now the Yorkshire Building Society, was part of the 1786 classical rebuilding of the street when all the buildings were faced in stucco. The building on the corner of Castle Street and Derby Square was originally built for the **South Wales Bank.** It was designed by **Lucy and Littler** and opened in 1868. Note the Corinthian capitals at the top of the building, cheekily adapted to contain Liver Birds.

Harrington Street once contained **John Sadler's** premises. Sadler perfected a method of printing on pottery in the early 1750s. He rapidly built up an extensive trade in printing on earthenware tiles and vessels. It was a virtual monopoly for many years and Josiah Wedgwood sent some of his wares to Sadler for printing.

The former **Bank of England,** now the **Trustee Savings Bank,** closes the vista to Brunswick Street. It was completed in 1848 and designed by **Professor C. R. Cockerell.** It is considered one of his best works. In 1883, the local Bank of England agent, **T. F. Agnew,** and an associate **Samuel Smith,** founded the first British, *'Society for the Prevention of Cruelty to Children'* in Liverpool after he returned from a visit to New York's pioneering society.

The **Co-operative Bank,** originally the **Adelphi Bank,** was designed by **W. D. Caroe** and completed in 1892. It is a granite and sandstone building and has an unusual copper *'onion'* dome. The bronze doors sculpted by **Stirling Lee** show four panels of historical pairs of inseparable friends – *'Achilles and Patroclus', 'David and Jonathan', 'Roland and Oliver'* and *'Castor and Pollux'.*

A nineteenth century impression of Liverpool Castle by E. W. Cox

The following year **Prince Rupert** led an army of 10,000 soldiers to fight the Roundheads in Liverpool. The castle eventually fell after 1,800 of Prince Rupert's troops were killed. Later **Colonel Birch** became governor and, during the Commonwealth and Protectorate rule, Liverpool underwent a period of recovery. The castle fell into disuse and was finally demolished in 1721 to make way for **St George's Church,** itself demolished in 1897.

It was decided to build a **Victoria Monument** after the Queen's death in 1901, and the present structure was designed by **F. M. Simpson,** the first Professor of Architecture at Liverpool University. The sculptor was **Charles Allen,** the Vice-Principal of the Municipal School of Art. The four bronze groups represent *'Agriculture', 'Commerce', 'Education'* and *'Industry'* and there is a plaque recording the site of Liverpool Castle.

The Queen's statue was unveiled in 1906 by **Princess Louise,** Queen Victoria's daughter. A competent sculptor herself, she is reported to have said, *'Surely Mama never looked like that'.* **King Edward VII,** however, thought it a good likeness.

Castle Moat House, on the north side of the square, was completed in 1840 and was designed by **Edward Corbett** for the North and South Wales Bank. Behind it lies **Castle**

Former Adelphi Bank

SANCTUARY STONE; THE SEVEN ORIGINAL STREETS OF LIVERPOOL.

No. 20 Castle Street has a plaque which draws attention to the **Sanctuary Stone** embedded in the road some nine metres (30') away. This is the only stone marking the boundary of the old Liverpool Fair to have survived. Another one was once to be found in Dale Street. The fair was held on 25th July and 11th November. Between these two stones, for 10 days before and after each fair, debtors might walk free from arrest provided they were engaged in lawful business. The privilege was cancelled by an Act of 1696.

Sir James Picton said that – *'The history of Castle Street is the history of Liverpool',* and this fine street still remains the identifiable centre of the city. The streets of the town were laid out at the beginning of the 13th century, the seven original ones being Dale Street and Water Street, Tithebarn Street and Chapel Street running east to west, and Old Hall Street, High Street and Castle Street running north to south. Today, Castle Street is one of the most sumptuous Victorian streets in Britain and a fitting setting for the Town Hall.

TOWN HALL.

The **Town Hall,** built between 1749 and 1754, is the city's third and was designed by **John Wood the Elder of Bath (1704-1754).** The ground floor was originally open and was intended to act as an exchange for merchants to transact business, with the upper floor being used for civic purposes. The building was severely damaged by fire in 1795 – the main water supplies were frozen and firemen were unable to use their hoses.

Town Hall

James Wyatt was commissioned to reconstruct the building. He added the impressive dome on its high drum and later, with **John Foster senior,** added the two-storey Corinthian portico. Minerva is located on top of the dome but her shield incorporates the Union Jack! Note the animal sculptures round the building representing countries with which Liverpool traded. The interiors were not finished until 1820, but together they form an exceptionally fine suite of late Georgian design.

The building has been subject to attack at least three times: in 1775 seamen protesting against the reduction in their wages attacked it with cannon and in 1881 there was an abortive attempt by the Fenians to blow it up. War damage, following a raid in June 1941, was more serious, but since then it has been restored.

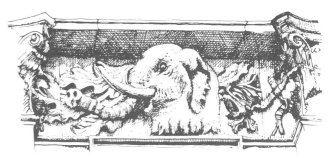

Town Hall Animal Wall Sculpture

Many famous people have visited the building and appeared on the entrance balcony. **King Edward VII** is reported to have been very impressed with the interiors, comparing them favourably with those at the Winter Palace in St Petersburg. **Mark Twain** was the principal guest at a special banquet held in 1907 to mark the city's 700th birthday. At the height of Beatlemania in 1964 the **Beatles** were received by the Lord Mayor and appeared on the Town Hall balcony to be seen by many thousands of people in the adjacent streets.

The view looking west down Water Street is magnificent, enclosed as it is by high buildings which are of great quality. The Royal Liver Building and Liver Birds are visible at the bottom with the river beyond. It is one of Europe's great street views.

LIVERPOOL INSURANCE COMPANIES: ABORTIVE PROPOSAL FOR A CONFEDERATE CLUB.

This area contains a number of buildings that have for many years been associated with insurance companies, although some of them now have different uses. The impressive former **Liverpool and London Chambers,** now housing the **Royal Bank of Scotland,** was completed in 1856 and designed by **Professor C. R. Cockerell. Professor Reilly,** the noted Professor of Architecture at Liverpool University, said of the entrance that: *'There is no more original and at the same time satisfactory public door in England'.* The building occupies the site of Liverpool's first Town Hall which was located here c. 1523-1673.

Also impressive is the **Queen Insurance Building** on the south side of Dale Street in **Queen Avenue.** It was designed by **Samuel Rowland** and completed in 1839 for

Queen Avenue

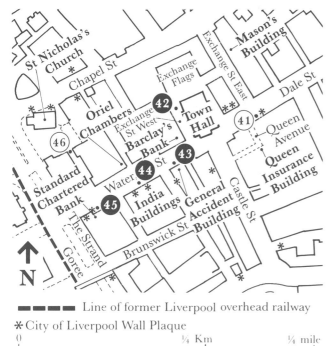

down from the balcony of the Town Hall at the merchants assembled below, she is reputed to have remarked that she had never before seen so large a number of well dressed gentlemen collected together in one place.

The **Nelson Monument** in the middle of the Flags was Liverpool's first piece of outdoor public sculpture and was erected in 1813. It was designed by **Matthew Cotes Wyatt** and the sculptor was **Richard Westmacott junior.** It shows Nelson receiving the Trafalgar battle honour from the Goddess of Victory in the form of a crown placed on his uplifted sword. Three other crowns are visible representing the Battles of the Nile, Copenhagen and St Vincent. Nelson's death is depicted in the form of a skeleton hand on his heart. At the rear Britannia weeps.

The four figures at the base depict **French** prisoners of war taken at the four battles. When **Herman Melville (1819-1891),** the **American** author, visited Liverpool in 1839 he mistook them for African slaves and had to be corrected. Herman Melville's most famous work was *'Moby Dick',* but he also wrote a lengthy autobiographical novel entitled *'Redburn'.* This recalled his impressions of Liverpool as a poor friendless sailor aged 19 years.

The **two telephone kiosks** on the east side of **Exchange Street West** are *'listed'* by the Department of the Environment as of *'special architectural or historic interest'* and are to remain here. They were designed by **Sir Giles Gilbert Scott,** the architect of Liverpool Cathedral, for national use. The K2 type which is the larger one, was designed in 1924 and is now extremely rare. The K6 type was designed in 1936 and, although less rare, is still not commonly found.

Barclays Bank, formerly **Martin's Bank,** stands on the west side of **Exchange Street West.** A plaque at the building's base in this street recalls the fact that 4,719 boxes of gold weighing approximately 284 tonnes (280 tons) were stored here prior to being shipped to Canada during the Second World War. When France collapsed in 1940, the Government decided that the Bank of England's gold reserves should be moved away from London. Part of the reserves were brought to Liverpool and stored in the vast strong rooms in the basement of this building.

the Royal Bank. The Dale Street facade carries the coat of arms of the Royal Bank on its top balustrade prominent against the sky.

The Liverpool and London and Globe Insurance Company, the Queen Insurance Company and the Royal Insurance Company – all Liverpool companies – together with the London-based London Insurance Company, were the only companies that paid in full the claims made upon them by policy holders affected by the San Francisco earthquake of 1906.

Liverpool insurance underwriters bore the brunt of the catastrophes, not only of the San Francisco earthquake but also the Great Fire of Chicago of 1871, without legal obligation and earned a reputation second to none. The Liverpool Underwriters Association, founded in 1803, is the oldest in the world.

Exchange Street East was, until the 1970's, the home of the **Liverpool Stock Exchange.** The Exchange started in the 1830's, in a coffee house near St Nicholas's Church patronised by leaders of commerce.

Mason's Building was built in 1868. The site was originally intended to have a *'Confederate Club'* built on it for the Liverpool merchants who were supporters of the Confederate cause and had trading connections with the southern states. When the Civil War turned against the Confederates the project was abandoned and the present building erected.

At the time of the Civil War one **American** visitor to Liverpool wrote home that: *'There are more Confederate flags flying in Liverpool than in Richmond.'*

EXCHANGE FLAGS; NELSON MONUMENT; HERMAN MELVILLE; TELEPHONE KIOSKS; BANK OF ENGLAND GOLD RESERVES.

Exchange Flags takes its name from the flagstones that used to cover the square. It originally covered a bonded warehouse and the monument in the middle acted as a ventilator. Underground car parks are now located under the Flags. The Town Hall forms the south side of the square.

In the 19th century Exchange Flags formed an open air exchange floor and when, in 1851, **Queen Victoria** looked

MARTINS BANK HEAD OFFICE; GENERAL ACCIDENT BUILDING; MAJOR GENERAL SIR BANASTRE TARLETON

Barclay's Bank, originally the head office of **Martin's Bank,** was completed in 1932 and was

Barclays Bank

designed by the Liverpool architect, **Herbert J. Rowse (1887-1963).** It is his most lavish work. It was technically very advanced for its time with completely ducted pipes and cables and low temperature ceiling heating. The sculpture is by **H. Tyson Smith (1880-1972)** and the whole ensemble is one of the most impressive commercial buildings of its time.

The **General Accident Building** was formerly the **Bank of Liverpool head office** and was completed in 1899. The great bronze entrance doors have sculpted tigers' heads with open mouths and ferocious teeth. **Lascars, Indian** seamen, from an area containing man-eating tigers, would rub the teeth for luck when in Liverpool.

The site of the **General Accident Building** once contained the birthplace of **Major General Sir Banastre Tarleton, Bt M.P. (1754-1833).** He was a great national hero, and tried when only in his twenties to quell the rebellion in the battles of Charleston, Philadelphia and New York before being finally captured by Washington at Yorktown in 1781.

Oriel Chambers

Banastre Tarleton

In the 18th century **Water Street** was a fashionable place of residence for wealthy Liverpool merchants. It also contained the *'Golden Talbot'* – a coaching inn. It is now one of the finest commercial streets in Liverpool.

*INDIA BUILDINGS;
ORIEL CHAMBERS; PETER ELLIS;
JOHN WELLBORN ROOT.*

The majestic **India Buildings** were designed by **Herbert J. Rowse,** with **Briggs and Thornely,** and completed in 1931. The present building incorporates the site of the first India Buildings erected in 1837-9 by **George Holt.**

Oriel Chambers, on the north side of Water Street, was completed in 1864 and designed by the Liverpool architect **Peter Ellis (1804-1884).** It is one of the most significant buildings of its date in Europe and is a pioneer in the use of cast iron construction. The vaulted brick floors are

supported on cast iron columns, and the facades to Water Street and Covent Garden have oriel windows picking up every ray of light from the canyon-like streets.

The building, when completed, was called *'A great abortion'* and *'An agglomeration of plate glass bubbles'.* Ellis completed another pioneering building, using cast iron construction and large areas of external glass at No. 16 Cook Street in 1866. The technical virtuosity of these two buildings was not lost on a young **American** in Liverpool at that time.

John Wellborn Root (1850-1891) was born in Lumpkin, Georgia and was aged 11 at the outbreak of the Civil War. The dangerous conditions of the war concerned Root's father and he sent his son to the safety of Liverpool.

The expatriate American spent two years at school in Wallasey and visited Liverpool often. Later, after his return to America, he became a partner in the architectural firm of Burnham and Root. This great Chicago practice designed many buildings in that city, including the Monadnock Building, one of the most celebrated of the early skyscrapers. This building utilised a large amount of glass to admit as much light as possible from the dark street outside. Peter Ellis's work in Liverpool is said to have made a big impression on John Root.

*CAPTAIN DAWSON; PRIVATEERING;
FORTUNATUS WRIGHT; WILLIAM
HUTCHINSON.*

The **Standard Chartered Bank** occupies a site on which stood one of Liverpool's Custom Houses between 1680 and 1722. Adjacent to the site was the home, in the 18th century, of **Captain Dawson,** a successful privateer. In 1778, aboard the Liverpool ship *'Mentor',* he captured the French East Indian *'Carnatic'.* This was the most valuable prize ever brought into Liverpool as it contained spices and diamonds valued at £135,000.

In the 18th and early 19th centuries, after licensing by *'letters of marque'* granted by the Government, ships could be fitted out to waylay enemy ships for personal and for the town's profit. The most famous Liverpool privateer was **Fortunatus Wright,** who died in 1757. He became a national figure due to his reputation for attacking French ships, particularly in the Mediterranean. He helped establish the image of Liverpool as being the home of daring and courageous seafarers.

William Hutchinson was another Liverpool privateer who served with Fortunatus Wright. He was the founder of

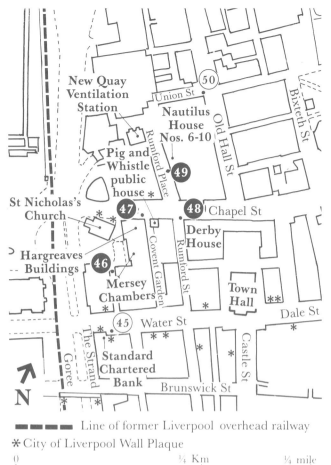

New Quay Ventilation Station
Nautilus House Nos. 6-10
Pig and Whistle public house
St Nicholas's Church
Hargreaves Buildings
Mersey Chambers
Standard Chartered Bank
Derby House
Town Hall

Union St
Old Hall St
Bixteth St
Chapel St
Rumford Place
Covent Garden
Rumford St
Water St
Dale St
Castle St
Brunswick St
The Strand
Goree

━━━━ Line of former Liverpool overhead railway

✱ City of Liverpool Wall Plaque

0   ¼ Km   ¼ mile

Scale

A Liverpool Privateer in the Mersey in 1797

the *'Marine Society',* a boatbuilder and a authoritative author of a book on naval architecture. He was also the inventor of reflecting mirrors for lighthouses, the first one in the world being at Bidston, Wirral in 1763. In addition he observed tides, weather and winds in order to incorporate them in tables.

MERSEY CHAMBERS; CHURCH OF OUR LADY AND ST NICHOLAS; COLONEL ROBERT BROADNEAUX.

Mersey Chambers, designed by **George Grayson (c 1834-1912),** was built in 1877 for T and J Harrison. The **Churchyard** was laid out as a public garden in 1891 in memory of James Harrison, a partner in the firm of shipowners.

There has been a church on the site of the present **Church of Our Lady and St Nicholas** since the 13th century. For many centuries this was a Chapel of Ease to St Mary's, Walton, which was then Liverpool's parish church. St. Nicholas's now undertakes this function. The present tower was designed by **Thomas Harrison** of Chester and was completed in 1815. It replaced a previous tower which collapsed in 1810, killing 25 people at prayer. The present nave was built in 1952 replacing an earlier structure destroyed in the Second World War.

Church of our Lady and St Nicholas S. Long

The church is known as the *'Sailors' Church',* St Nicholas being the patron saint of sailors, and the tower is a landmark visible from the river. Originally the Mersey lapped at the foot of the churchyard until the river was pushed back to accommodate the present road area and dock system.

Colonel Robert Broadneaux (1617-1727) was buried in the original graveyard surrounding the church. He was a Lieutenant in the reign of Charles I, a Captain of Horse and Gentleman of the Bedchamber to Oliver Cromwell, and a Lieutenant Colonel under William III. At the age of 83, being attacked by a sickness he thought fatal, he ordered his coffin. He recovered and slept nightly in his coffin for 26 years till the time of his death. He retained his memory to the end.

On the north side of the church, fronting Chapel Street, is a modern metal sculpture depicting *'Christ upon an Ass'.* It was sculpted by **Brian Burgess,** the Liverpool born artist, and erected in 1971.

HARGREAVES BUILDINGS; CHRISTOPHER COLUMBUS; SIR WILLIAM BROWN; SIR JAMES PICTON.

Hargreaves Buildings now houses the **Liverpool Racquet Club.** It is in the style of a Venetian palazzo with round arched windows on the main floor. In the roundels of the windows are busts of historical figures connected with Central America. Christopher Columbus, the navigator and explorer, is depicted, as is Queen Anacoana, the Queen of the Maguana, a tribe in the West Indies.

There is a statue of **Christopher Columbus (1451-1506)** by the Palm House in Sefton Park, Liverpool and on Columbus Day every year the **Anglo-Ibero-American Society** have a wreath-laying ceremony at the statue. It is believed that the statue is the only one of Columbus in Britain. The beginnings of Liverpool's growth as a trading port are to be found after the first recorded cargo from America was received in 1648.

Sir William Brown, the owner of Hargreaves Buildings, was born in Ireland. At the age of 16 he was taken to **America,** where his father established a prosperous firm of merchants known as Brown Bros. and Harrison in Baltimore. Aged 25 years, he was despatched to establish a branch of his father's firm in Liverpool. He was a shrewd man and became an extremely prosperous merchant and banker much involved with the commercial, cultural and civic life of Liverpool. In 1857, on Liverpool's 650th birthday, he laid the foundation stone for the William Brown Library in the street named after him.

Sir James Picton (1805-1889), the designer of Hargreaves Buildings, left school aged 13 years to work in the family timber yard. In 1826 he became an assistant surveyor and later prospered as an architect, surveyor and valuer. He was the chairman of the town's Libraries Committee for 40 years and the Picton Library is named after him. At the age of 60 he retired and devoted his life to literature, scholarship and public life. Sir James's finest literary work is his two volume *'Memorials of Liverpool'*, which is a source of greatly valued informaton on the history of the city. He designed many important buildings in Liverpool, the best remaining possibly being Hargreaves Buildings.

The **Pig and Whistle public house** was built in the early 19th century and was originally used as an hotel, beefsteak, tripe and chop house. The entrance was until recently embellished with a brass plaque bearing the words *'Emigrants supplied'.* The plaque has now been removed to the safety of the interior. The building was one of many such hostelries that sold provisions to emigrants passing through Liverpool.

COMBINED H.Q. OF THE WESTERN APPROACHES; SECOND WORLD WAR BOMB DAMAGE IN LIVERPOOL.

The large office block on the corner of Rumford Street and Chapel Street is called **Derby House.** On the corner is a plaque recording the fact that during the Second World War the **Combined Headquarters of the Western Approaches** was situated below this building. The accommodation in the basement area was fortified and became known as *'The Citadel'.* The movement of ships, submarines and aircraft was plotted on great wall charts and tables, and here top secret signals were transmitted and received.

Liverpool paid dearly for its honourable and important role in the war. As the western gateway for supplies and vast troop movements by sea, it received great attention from the Luftwaffe and was Hitler's chief target outside London. Between July 1940 and January 1942, in 68 raids by German bombers, 3,966 people were killed. Property losses ran into millions of pounds and the chief targets were the docks and railways. In addition, swathes of Liverpool's city centre were damaged and the area between Paradise Street and Derby Square resembled a brick field.

Nearly 200,000 houses were destroyed or damaged, and it is probable that Merseyside sustained more damage and casualties relative to its size than any other area in Britain outside London.

AMERICAN CIVIL WAR; JAMES DUNWOODY BULLOCH; CONFEDERATE EMBASSY IN ENGLAND; C.S.S. 'ALABAMA'; J. A. BRODIE.

In 1861, at the time of the **American** Civil War, a Georgian born ex-U.S. Navy Lieutenant named **James Dunwoody Bulloch,** a Confederate agent, arrived in Liverpool. He came under cover of the Southern Cotton Commissioners to order Confederate ships from various shipyards in England, including Merseyside. He commenced his operations at **Nautilus House, Nos. 6-10 Rumford Place,** an office building built in the 1840s on the east side of the street. The building was in effect the Confederate Embassy in England.

James Dunwoody Bulloch

Within months of arrival in 1861 he had signed contracts with local shipbuilders resulting, with other commissions, in the building of two cruisers – the C.S.S. *'Florida'* and the C.S.S. *'Alabama'* – which wrought havoc with Yankee shipping. The *'Alabama',* built by Lairds of Birkenhead, sunk 68 Yankee ships on the oceans of the world before being sunk herself. No other ship in any navy or war has sunk so many ships.

C.S.S. "Alabama"

Bulloch masterminded the building of a further 37 Confederate blockade runners by Merseyside shipyards. There was a large amount of sympathy for the Confederate cause in Liverpool and Lancashire owing to the close cotton trading connections with the southern states, and this caused much resentment with the northern states. This in turn caused considerable embarrassment to the British Government which put pressure to bear on Liverpool, mostly unsuccessfully, to desist.

Perhaps sensibly, James Dunwoody Bulloch made Liverpool his permanent home and was buried in Toxteth Cemetery. **Fraser Trenholme & Co.,** who were foreign bankers to the Confederacy, also had their offices at Nos. 6-10 Rumford Place and worked closely with Bulloch.

The **New Quay Ventilation Station,** attached to the dock branch of the Mersey Road Tunnel, was designed by

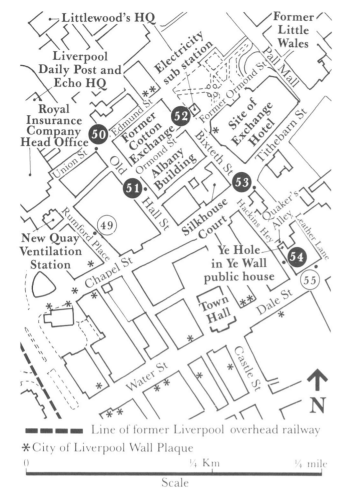

Littlewood's HQ · Former Little Wales · Liverpool Daily Post and Echo HQ · Electricity sub station · Former Ormond St · Pall Mall · Royal Insurance Company Head Office · **50** · Edmund St · Former Cotton Exchange · **52** · Ormond St · Site of Exchange Hotel · Albany Building · Bixteth St · Tithebarn St · **51** · Hall St · **53** · Old Hall St · Silkhouse Court · Hackins Hey · Quaker's Alley · Leather Lane · **49** · Rumford Place · New Quay Ventilation Station · Chapel St · Ye Hole in Ye Wall public house · **54** · **55** · Town Hall · Dale St · Water St · Castle St

N

▬ ▬ ▬ Line of former Liverpool overhead railway

✳ City of Liverpool Wall Plaque

0 .... ¼ Km .... ¼ mile

Scale

the City Engineer, **J. A. Brodie,** and other consultants. It is in brick with copper coving in a style of architecture derived from Wilhelm Dudok, a Dutch architect.

J. A. Brodie, the Liverpool City Engineer from 1898 to 1926, was instrumental in laying out many of the dual carriageways that serve Liverpool. These include Queens Drive and Brodie Avenue, the latter named after him. His expertise was so valued that the British Government requested him to design the road system for New Delhi in association with Sir Edwin Lutyens, the architect. He also invented the use of nets for football goal posts.

ROYAL INSURANCE COMPANY; LIVERPOOL DAILY POST & ECHO; OLD HALL; COTTON EXCHANGE; JOHN NEWTON.

The large sand-coloured office block to the north west is the head office of the **Royal Insurance Company,** which was founded in Liverpool in 1845. It is one of the largest fire, accident and marine insurance companies in the world. Next to it, to the north, is the head office of the **Liverpool Daily Post & Echo** newspapers, which serve not only Liverpool, but Merseyside and large areas of Lancashire, Cheshire and North Wales.

In the vicinity of the north west corner of Union Street and Old Hall Street is the site of the former **Old Hall,** a 13th century mansion which was the seat of the **Moore** family. The family dominated Liverpool for over 400 years and provided 40 mayors as well as several M.P.s.

The modern building to the east was built in the 1960s and replaced the main facade of the **Edwardian Cotton Exchange,** which was completed in 1906. The two stone figures at the front were taken from the former facade and represent *'Science'* and *'Industry and Commerce'.*

Liverpool first handled cotton in 1709 and in the 19th century merchants sold cotton in the open air on Exchange Flags behind the Town Hall. Trading reached an all time peak in 1911 to 1912 when five million bales of the six million imported into Britain came through Liverpool. Until the last war the city was the greatest market in the world for the purchase and sale of *'spot'* cotton, as it served the huge Lancashire cotton industry. There is no longer a cotton exchange in Liverpool, but the Liverpool Cotton Association, founded in 1882 and located in **Cotton Exchange Buildings** in Edmund Street, acts as a forum and arbitration centre for traders throughout the world. It has members in 54 countries and even today 70% of the world's export of raw cotton is sold under *'Liverpool arbitration'.*

John Newton (1725-1807) lived in Edmund Street. He was the captain of a slave ship at the age of 24, a position he gave up when he suffered a bout of ill health four years later. He later recommended the abolition of slavery and assisted Wilberforce in his campaign. He became a clergyman and hymn writer and was the Vicar of Olney in Buckinghamshire. He wrote the Olney Hymns, the best known of which is *'How sweet the name of Jesus sounds.'* His most famous composition, however, is *'Amazing Grace'.*

John Newton

ALBANY BUILDING; THOMAS ARMSTRONG.

The **Albany Building** was built in 1856 for **Richard Naylor,** a wealthy Liverpool banker of Hooton Hall in the Wirral. It was designed by the London architect, **J. K. Colling.** It is one of the earliest large office buildings in the city and was designed to provide company offices with the cotton trade in mind. Around the spacious courtyard are basement rooms in which samples could be displayed. Before the Cotton Exchange was built next to it, it formed a meeting place for cotton brokers who rented the offices. Inside, single lock-up rooms open off top lit corridors which run the length of the building. Naylor's coat of arms can be seen on the wrought iron gates, and in the coffered ceiling of the vestibule is the monogram of Naylor and his wife Mary Sophia. **Thomas Armstrong,** the novelist and author of *'King Cotton',* worked in one of these offices as a young man.

GEORGE STUBBS; LITTLEWOODS AND VERNONS; 'LITTLE WALES'.

George Stubbs (1724-1806), the artist and anatomist, was born in Liverpool. His exact birthplace is not known, but it

34

George Stubbs

may have been over the workshop of his father, a leather finisher and seller, in Ormond Street. He certainly lived here as a youth, roughly on the site of the present electricity sub-station.

Stubbs had little formal artistic training and was a self-taught painter. He was interested in anatomical science and dissected the bodies of animals as well as human beings. By 1745 he was a noted provincial portrait painter and was studying anatomy in York. In 1766 he published the *'Anatomy of the Horse'* and was elected an Associate of the Royal Academy in 1780.

He witnessed the golden age of horse racing and obtained many commissions for paintings of horses from the aristocracy and the newly affluent middle class. In addition he painted lions, tigers, dogs and other animals. His knowledge of anatomy resulted in superbly accurate paintings. He is represented in all the national collections, and the Royal Family own many examples of his work. The Walker Art Gallery in Liverpool and the Lady Lever Art Gallery in the Wirral together hold the largest public collection of Stubbs' work in Britain.

The large glass office block to the north is the headquarters of the **Littlewood's Organisation,** the department store, mail order and football pools organisation. **Littlewood's** and **Vernon's** together make Liverpool Britain's football pool centre. Both organisations seized on an idea of the 1920s and grew rapidly, particularly during the lean years of the 1930s. The organisations now employ thousands of people, and Littlewoods is reputed to be the largest privately owned concern in Britain.

Looking north east beyond the present modern office complex is **Pall Mall.** This street and its side streets were known in the 19th century as *'Little Wales'.* The first Welsh Chapel was built here in 1787, and by 1813, one in every ten persons in Liverpool was of Welsh origin. Many of them could only speak Welsh! The National Eisteddfod was held in Liverpool in 1840, 1851, 1884, 1900 and 1929.

FORMER EXCHANGE STATION; MAYORS AND LORD MAYORS OF LIVERPOOL; COAT OF ARMS OF LIVERPOOL.

The modern office block named **Silkhouse Court** is on the site of a silk factory built by an Italian concern. It was possibly the first factory in Liverpool. Other old Liverpool trades were watchmaking, pottery, furniture making and sugar and salt refining, but most have now gone.

The stone facade of the former **Exchange Hotel,** now **Mercury Court,** dominates this area. The hotel was built

in 1886 and designed by **Henry Shelmerdine** for the Lancashire & Yorkshire Railway Company. The facade has been retained to *'front'* a large new office block to the rear. The two arches were formerly the carriage entrances to the station and now lead to a glazed atrium and the offices. Between the arches a bronze medallion of **John Pearson** may be seen. Mr. Pearson was the Chairman of the Company and Mayor of Liverpool from 1871 to 1872.

There were Mayors of Liverpool between 1207 and 1291, but no names are recorded. The first recorded name in the Town Hall is **John de More (1292-1293).** The first Lord Mayor was **Robert Durning Holt** in 1893 after Liverpool became a city in 1880. The first woman Lord Mayor was **Margaret Beavan (1877-1931),** in 1927. She was a tireless worker for children and mothers on Merseyside. In 1907 she founded the Liverpool Child Welfare Association.

Liverpool's coat of arms is made up of a shield incorporating a cormorant with seaweed or laver in its mouth. Above this is another cormorant, again with seaweed in its mouth. To the left is Neptune, his waist wreathed in seaweed and on his head an eastern gold crown. Neptune carries a trident in his right hand and a supported banner in his left incorporating the arms of Liverpool. To the right is a Triton, again his waist wreathed in seaweed and blowing a shell. Triton's right hand supports a banner showing a ship under sail.

City of Liverpool Coat of Arms

The civic motto below the coat of arms *DEUS NOBIS HAEC OTIA FECIT* was taken from a line of Virgil's Eclogues, which translated means *'God has bestowed these blessings on us'.*

It is probable that **James, the 10th Earl of Derby from 1702 to 1736,** suggested the motto to the Town Council.

HACKINS HEY; QUAKER MEETING HOUSE; YE HOLE IN YE WALL PUBLIC HOUSE; LEATHER LANE.

Hackins Hey is one of Liverpool's mediaeval streets. *'Hey'* is an anglicisation of the French word *'Haie',* meaning an enclosed field, and there was such a field here owned by **John Hacking** in the 17th century. *'Hey'* later came to mean, especially in Liverpool, a small lane such as this one.

A **Friends Meeting House** was erected at the corner of **Quakers Alley** and **Hackins Hey** in 1706, and attached to it was a burial ground. A Quaker School was built adjacent to the Meeting House in 1752. The Quakers left the area in 1796 for Hunter Street. **'Ye Hole in Ye Wall' public house** was built near the site of the former Meeting House. It is reputed to be the oldest public house in Liverpool and, until the passing of the Sex Discrimination Act 1975, it admitted only male patrons.

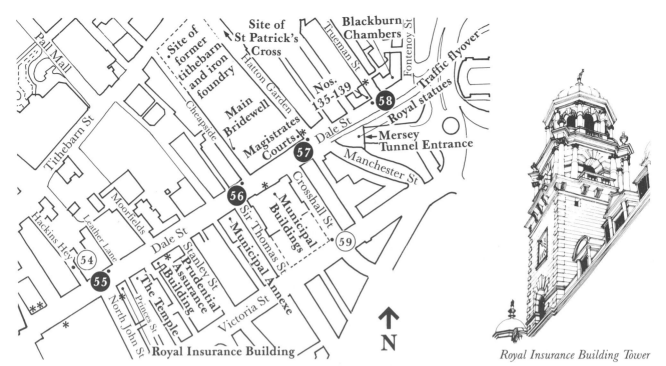

Royal Insurance Building Tower

✱ City of Liverpool Wall Plaque

0   ¼ Km   ¼ mile
Scale

Leather Lane, running parallel to Hackins Hey to the east, once led to Leather Hall, which was located near Pall Mall. Here animal skins were imported and traded.

Leather Lane

55

ROYAL INSURANCE BUILDING; THE TEMPLE; PRUDENTIAL ASSURANCE BUILDING; ALFRED WATERHOUSE.

A number of handsome Victorian and Edwardian office buildings are visible from this point. The **Royal Insurance Building** was completed in 1903 and was designed by **J. Francis Doyle,** a Liverpool architect. Below its golden dome on the main body of the building, a frieze of figures depicting links with insurance runs round three sides of the building. Over the entrance in North John Street *'Invention'* is shown giving on the one hand the means of saving life from fire, and on the other the means of saving property. The centre Dale Street panel shows *'Mercury God of Commerce'* causing the elements to pour water on the flame enveloped world. The right hand panel shows the *'Arts'* and the left hand the *'Sciences'.* The Princes Street panel depicts *'Wisdom'* and *'Prudence'* comforting the fatherless, and counselling youth and entrusting old age to the care of commerce. All the sculpture is by **C. J. Allen** of the Liverpool School of Art.

The Temple, next to the Royal Insurance Building, was designed by **Sir James Picton** for **Sir William Brown** and erected in 1864 to 1865. Over the window above the main entrance are the arms of the Brown family. The Latin motto reads *'Harmony becomes brothers',* an allusion to the four sons of the Irish merchant Alexander Brown, of whom Sir William was one, who were in partnership with him. In the shield can be seen four hands clasped together.

Next to the Temple eastwards is the **Prudential Assurance Building** by **Alfred Waterhouse (1830-1905),** which was completed in 1886. The tower was added later by his son. Waterhouse was born in Liverpool and later had one of the largest and most prestigious architectural practices in London.

Prudential Assurance Building

DALE STREET AND STAGE COACHES; MUNICIPAL ANNEXE; MUNICIPAL BUILDINGS; MAIN BRIDEWELL.

Prior to the coming of the railways, Liverpool's contact with the rest of the country was by stage coach. **Dale Street** contained the largest number of inns, hotels and eating houses devoted to this traffic. Stage coaches to and from Manchester and London left from Dale Street, which also served travellers using the Dublin packet. The most famous inn was the *'Saracen's Head'* situated, between 1810 and 1853, on part of the site now occupied by the Municipal Buildings. Thirty coaches a day called here.

The **Municipal Annexe,** on the west corner of Dale Street and Sir Thomas Street, was originally the Conservative Club. It was completed in 1883 and designed by **F. & G. Holme.** It was taken over for municipal offices and committee rooms between the two world wars.

The **Municipal Buildings** were completed in 1866 and designed by **John Weightman.** In a mixture of French and Italian Renaissance styles, they boast 16 fine external sculptured figures and a large number of Corinthian columns, no two capitals of which are the same. The tower contains, in addition to the clock bell, four bells which are rung on special occasions such as the Queen's Birthday (actual and official), St George's Day, Remembrance Day and whilst royalty are present in the city centre.

Municipal Buildings and Annexe

The **Main Bridewell,** a few steps up Cheapside, was completed in 1864 and was designed by **John Weightman.** It is the principal police premises for the reception and detention of prisoners in Liverpool, and for those due to appear at the adjoining Magistrates' Courts. Liverpool in 1836 was one of the first towns in England to form a police force.

JOHN WYKE; ST PATRICK'S CROSS; MERSEY IRON FOUNDRY; JOHN CRAGG.

The **Magistrates' Courts,** completed in 1859 and designed by **John Weightman,** occupy the corner of Dale Street and Hatton Garden. Part of the site was once occupied by Wyke's Court, named after **John Wyke** from Prescot, who introduced watchmaking to Liverpool. He died in 1787 and is buried in Prescot Church.

At the northern end of **Hatton Garden** is the site of the former **St. Patrick's Cross.** This was recorded on old

maps, the earliest dating back to 1559. The last reference to it was made in 1786, and it would appear that it was dismantled or demolished after that date. The tradition is that the Cross marked the spot where **St Patrick** in 430 AD preached before sailing to convert the pagan Irish. Historically, St Patrick is said to have been born either in Wales, or even Scotland, but not in Ireland, and it is intriguing to find that Liverpool claims a relationship to the good saint. The tradition has persisted, and the **Holy Cross Roman Catholic Church** was erected in the mid 19th century near to the spot where the cross was said to have been.

A **tithebarn** originally owned by **Lord Molyneux** stood on **Tithebarn Street** until the beginning of the 19th century. The **Mersey Iron Foundry** was built behind the barn a few years before its demolition. The principal owner of this was **John Cragg (1767-1854).** He introduced cast iron construction to various types of building, including churches. St George's, Everton and St Michael's in the Hamlet, designed by **Thomas Rickman (1776-1841),** utilise cast iron from the foundry. The foundry also produced cast iron for export, and it is likely that many a church and verandah of the early 19th century in Australia, New Zealand, Africa and India, originated in Liverpool.

Nos. 135-139 DALE STREET; ROBERT MORRIS THE AMERICAN PATRIOT; STATUES OF KING GEORGE V AND QUEEN MARY.

Nos. 135-139 Dale Street are a terrace of late 18th century houses. **No. 139,** which also has a frontage to Trueman Street, was built for **John Houghton,** a distiller whose works were adjacent. On the Trueman Street elevation is a Venetian window with Adam style decoration and a fine tripartite doorway. It is the best surviving Liverpool merchant's house of the 18th century.

Blackburn Chambers occupies a site that formerly contained **Chorley Court,** which was a small street. **Robert Morris (1734-1806),** the **American** patriot and a signatory of the Declaration of Independence, was born here. After a poverty stricken childhood, he set sail for America when only 13. By the age of 20 he was a partner in a prosperous New York mercantile company.

Robert Morris

He is regarded as one of America's greatest early financiers and he almost single-handedly arranged the funding of the War of Independence. Afterwards he virtually controlled the operation of Congress. He became Superintendent of Finance, Head of the Navy Department and in Philadelphia he established the Bank of North America, the oldest financial institution in that country. He owned virtually the western half of New York State and much land in Virginia, South Carolina and Georgia. He died in a debtors' prison in Philadelphia following ruinous land speculations.

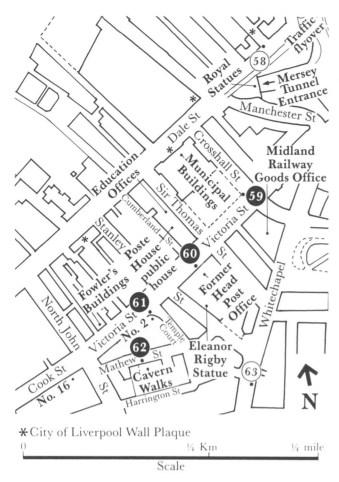

* City of Liverpool Wall Plaque

Scale

The walk to the next marker is rather circuitous by way of a path under the traffic flyover. Note the statues of **King George V** and **Queen Mary** by **Sir William Goscombe John** behind the Mersey Tunnel portal. They were originally sited at the two terminal features of the portal facing Dale Street, but had to be relocated when the flyover was built in the 1960s. King George V opened the **Mersey Tunnel** in 1934 and named it **Queensway** after his wife Queen Mary.

BEEHIVE PUBLIC HOUSE RAT PIT; MIDLAND RAILWAY GOODS OFFICE; SIR THOMAS JOHNSON; LIVERPOOL COMEDIANS.

The **Beehive public house** once stood in Crosshall Street and it had a rat pit at the rear. In 1853 *'Jenny Lind'*, a bull terrier, set up a record by killing 500 rats in 90 minutes.

The **Midland Railway Goods Office,** designed by **William Culshaw and Henry Sumners,** was completed in

Midland Railway Goods Office

1874 for the receipt and despatch of goods. The carved spandrels contain the shields of arms and carved names of towns served by the Midland Railway.

Sir Thomas Street was named after **Sir Thomas Johnson (1670-1729),** Liverpool's M.P. for 21 years. He was a leading figure behind the construction of Liverpool's, and indeed the world's, first commercial dock in 1715. He was engaged in the American tobacco trade but died in poverty in London.

Buildings in Sir Thomas Street with Education Offices at right

The **Education Offices** were designed by **C. E. Deacon** and completed in 1898. The pediment contains sculpture representing *'Knowledge personified'.* **Arthur Askey** worked for a time as a young clerk in the building, one of many Liverpool comedians to achieve national fame. Others include **Robb Wilton, Tommy Handley, Fred Emney, Ted Ray, Ken Dodd, Jimmy Tarbuck, Leonard Rossiter, Deryck Guyler** and **Derek Nimmo.**

DUKE OF CUMBERLAND; POSTE HOUSE PUBLIC HOUSE; PRINCE LOUIS NAPOLEON; WILLIAM MAKEPEACE THACKERAY; ELEANOR RIGBY SCULPTURE.

Cumberland Street is named in honour of **William Augustus, Duke of Cumberland,** During the 1745 Scottish Rebellion, the Duke was supported by the Liverpool Blues Regiment which served in the defence of Carlisle.

The **Poste House public house** in Cumberland Street is probably named after the poste horn, which was associated with coaching stations once prevalent in the area. The Post House had, in the 19th century, two very different well known patrons. **Prince Louis Napoleon (1808-1873),** visiting Merseyside to ride with the local hunts, once drank here. **William Makepeace Thackeray (1811-1863),** the novelist and author of *'Vanity Fair',* visited the inn when on a visit to Liverpool in 1852 to lecture at the old Philharmonic Hall.

The former **Head Post Office** was opened in 1899, but it suffered the indignity of having its top blown off in the Second World War. Despite this, it remained Liverpool's principal post office until the 1970s. During the 1930s records show that an average of 210,000 telegrams per week were handled in the building – a form of communication that has now disappeared with the growth of telephone ownership.

On the south western side of the former post office a **sculpture of Eleanor Rigby** may be found. This was sculpted by the pop singer **Tommy Steele** and erected in 1982. The name of Eleanor is taken from that of Eleanor Bron the actress and Rigby from a Bristol shop front name that **Paul McCartney** saw when visiting that city. Inside the bronze sculpture are the following items:—

a four leaf clover representing *'nature'*
a page of the Bible representing *'spiritual matters'*
a football sock representing *'leisure'*
a *'Dandy'* and *'Beano'* comic representing *'comedy'*
four sonnets representing *'romance'*.

VICTORIA STREET; FOWLER'S BUILDINGS; PETER ELLIS; NO. 16 COOK STREET.

Victoria Street was cut through this part of the city centre in 1867 to 1868 to improve traffic flow and produce a new and impressive location for commercial development. **No. 2 Temple Court** on the western side, which is faced in plaster, is an 18th century building pre-dating this civic improvement scheme.

Fowler's Buildings were designed by the noted Liverpool architect **Sir James Picton** and completed in 1864. The impressive stone front served as offices for the company, whilst behind the more functional structure served as a building in which to smoke fish then mainly exported to America. The Fowler family were keen members of the Salvation Army and established a number of residential buildings in Liverpool to serve needy people.

No. 16 Cook Street was designed by the Liverpool architect, **Peter Ellis (1804-1884),** and completed in 1866. Like his Oriel Chambers in Water Street completed two years earlier, it is a landmark in architecture. Its front

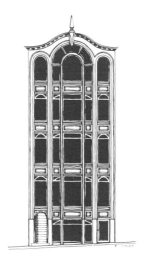

No. 16 Cook Street

elevation is composed of three giant bays in a Venetian window but filled in with plate glass. In the courtyard at the rear, squeezed into a corner against a wall of glass with cast iron mullions, is a glazed cast iron spiral staircase cantilevered from each floor. In its bare aesthetic style, it was a great advance for its time and heralded the 20th century modern movement in architecture.

When No. 16 Cook Street was nearing completion, the architectural magazine *'The Builder'* published a critique of Oriel Chambers damning it with such ferocity that from then on, Peter Ellis does not appear to have had any further architectural commissions.

CAVERN CLUB; THE BEATLES; OTHER "MERSEY SOUND" GROUPS; CAVERN WALKS; CYNTHIA LENNON; ARTHUR DOOLEY.

A Victorian warehouse that used to stand on the south side of Mathew Street became a jazz club in 1957, but later started to feature beat groups. The basement of the building was known as the **Cavern Club.** The **Beatles** played here nearly 300 times between March 1961 and August 1963. During this time **Cilla Black** was in charge of the cloakroom.

Many other musicians famous for the *'Mersey Sound'* performed in the Cavern, including the **Swinging Blue Jeans, Gerry and the Pacemakers, the Mojo's, the Undertakers, the Chessmen, the Searchers, Rory Storm and the Hurricanes, P. J. Proby, Billy J. Kramer** and the **Big Three.**

The Cavern closed in 1973 and the warehouse was demolished to enable an underground railway to be constructed. In 1984 the present building, known as **Cavern Walks,** designed by Liverpool architect **David Backhouse,** was opened on the site. It contains a rebuilding of the original Cavern Club in the basement, and shops, offices and an internal nine-storey atrium. The atrium contains a sculpture of the Beatles by **John Doubleday.** The external terracotta sculpture on the building is by **Cynthia Lennon, John Lennon's** first wife. The roses and doves represent *'Love'* and *'Peace'*. There is also an inscribed message from her to John Lennon near to the entrance of the Cavern Club.

'Rock and roll' music is firmly put in its place just by the site of one of its greatest shrines. In the brick paving of Mathew Street a manhole cover bears the inscription *'non-rocking'!*

On a building on the north side of Mathew Street is a **bronze sculpture** by the Liverpool Sculptor, **Arthur Dooley,** entitled: *'Four lads who shook the world'.* Mother Liverpool cradles three babies – John, George and Ringo – while a fourth, Paul, has grown *'Wings'* and flown away. The building to which it is affixed has no connection with the original Cavern Club.

On the terracotta keystone, at the top of the arched opening of the car park of Cavern Walks in Harrington Street, is a **gorilla applying lipstick** with the aid of a hand mirror. The sculpture is by **Hathernware Ltd.,** the terracotta manufacturers. A well known London architect who dislikes decoration on buildings stated that: *'Art is to architecture, like lipstick is to a gorilla'.* The Cavern Walks development contains much applied art, and its architect felt that this comment was so strange that it was worth recording visually.

The Beatles in 1964

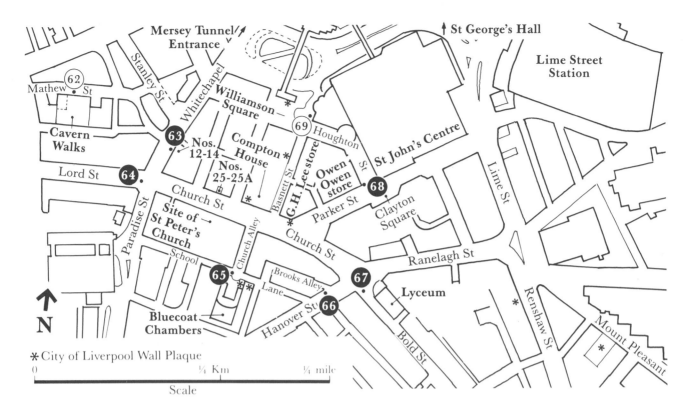

POOL OF LIVERPOOL; ORIGIN OF THE NAME 'LIVERPOOL'; NEMS STORES; BRIAN EPSTEIN.

Originally the **Pool of Liverpool** stretched from just north of the main entrance to the first Mersey Road Tunnel at Old Haymarket, down Whitechapel and Paradise Street, then turning west to connect with the Mersey between Canning Dock and Salthouse Dock. It was fed by Mosslake Brook, which drained the area of high ground to the east of the town centre. On the construction of Liverpool's first dock at what is now Canning Place, the Pool was culverted underground and the present streets were formed on top.

The **origin of the name of Liverpool** has baffled all investigators. The Liverpool historian **Sir James Picton**, in his *'Memorials of Liverpool',* states that it appears that the name originally applied to water rather than to land. The mouth of the stream in the town centre was called the *'Pool'* until the opening of the first dock in 1715. It is the first part of the name which gives difficulty. Many guesses have been made but none has met with general acceptance. The spelling has been tortured into many forms; no less than 40 variations have been given. It has finally settled down to very nearly the original spelling used in the Charter of King John in 1207, where it is spelt *'Liverpul'.*

Nos. 12-14 Whitechapel were once a branch of the **North End Music Stores (NEMS)**. These were owned by the Epstein family and managed by **Brian Epstein (1934-1967)**. In October 1961, he received many requests for the record *'My Bonnie'* which had been recorded in West Germany by a Liverpool group called the **Beatles**. He had not heard of the group or the record, but made enquiries and, as a result, went to the nearby Cavern Club to hear them performing. By December of that year he had become their manager.

'HOLY CORNER'; CHURCH STREET; FRANK WINFIELD WOOLWORTH; COMPTON HOUSE HOTEL.

This street junction has been called *'Holy Corner',* due to the religious connection of the names of the four thoroughfares which meet here – *'Whitechapel, Church Street, Paradise Street'* and *'Lord Street'.* The north east side used to be known as *'Bunney's Corner'* after the shop that once stood here. It sold continental and oriental goods and novelties.

Church Street was developed at the beginning of the 18th century and takes its name from the **Church of St. Peter** which was built parallel to it in 1704. The church was demolished in 1922 to enable the building now containing **'Top Shop'** to be built. A stone step from the Church containing a brass Maltese Cross is incorporated in the paving of the street.

Nos. 25-25A Church Street are interesting in that the **American, Frank Winfield Woolworth** opened his first shop in Europe here in 1909. On a wall above an adjacent roof may be seen the faded sign *'Woolworth's 3d and 6d store'.*

Marks & Spencer occupy **Compton House** which was designed by **Thomas Haigh** and erected in 1867 for Jeffrey's department store. This was Liverpool's most fascinating shop in the mid 19th century. It started in a single house and grew until it reached gigantic proportions. The shop was probably Liverpool's first department store. In 1865, owing to carelessness with a match, the shop was burned down and had to be rebuilt. It never regained its former prosperity and in 1871 the store closed. It was partly sub-divided into the Compton House Hotel, which was very popular with American transatlantic passengers. Carved in stonework on the corners of the Church Street elevation are the Royal Coat of Arms and those of the United States of America. Above the cornice is an unconventional version of Liverpool's Coat of Arms.

BLUECOAT CHAMBERS; EARLY GRAFFITI; THOMAS CREEVEY.

Bluecoat Chambers was originally built as a charity school in 1717. It is in a Queen Anne style. The inscription below the pediment reads,

'Dedicated to the promotion of Christian Charity and the training of poor boys in the principles of the Anglican Church. Founded this year of Salvation 1717.'

The building was paid for by **Bryan Blundell (1674-1756).** He was a tobacco merchant, privateer, slave trader and sea captain in the **American** trade. He not only transported slaves from Africa to the New World, but also servants and young children from Liverpool to be apprentices in the plantations.

The **Bluecoat School** remained here until 1906, when it moved out to more spacious premises in Wavertree. In 1909 the first **Lord Leverhulme, (1851-1925),** bought the building with the proceeds of a libel action he had won and intended to promote it as a centre for the arts. In 1914 a scheme was drawn up and then shelved due to the war. Nothing happened until 1927, when enthusiasts launched an appeal and bought it from Lord Leverhulme's executors. They formed the **Bluecoat Society of Arts,** which now owns the building.

It was damaged in the Second World War and a plaque in Latin over the entrance reads:

'Struck down from the sky by the firebrands of the enemy and partly destroyed on the 4th May 1941, restored with dutiful affection in the year 1951'.

Just inside the entrance gates on the north facade of the west block, some early graffiti may be seen – some initials dated 1796. A plaque on the southern facade of the Athenaeum Club opposite states that **Thomas Creevey M.P. (1786-1838),** diarist, was born in School Lane.

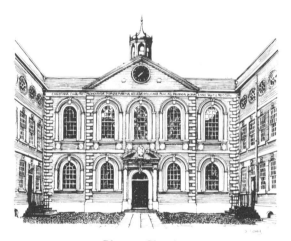

Bluecoat Chambers

HANOVER STREET; THE BROOKS FAMILY; FIRST INSTANT DRINK.

Hanover Street was probably named in honour of the **Duke of Cumberland,** King George II's brother. The Duke had honoured the town by a royal inspection in appreciation of Liverpool's support for his brother when the Scots rebelled in 1745.

Brooks Alley is named after **Joseph Brooks,** a builder, ropemaker and merchant who lived nearby in the mid 18th century. His relatives included Archdeacon Brooks and Major Edward Brooks who was killed in the last duel to take place in Liverpool in 1805. **Humphrey Brooke,** the Elizabethan privateer, is thought to have been a member of the same family. It is said that Humphrey Brooke discovered in 1588, the Spanish plan for an invincible *'Armada',* which he reported to Sir Francis Drake.

Further south, down **Hanover Street** on the south eastern side, were at one time the premises of **Ayrton Saunders and Company,** manufacturing chemists. The firm produced the first *'instant'* drink of tea, milk and sugar in tablet form for troops in the trenches in the First World War.

BOLD STREET; LYCEUM; DR. JAMES CURRIE.

Bold Street was originally a ropewalk for the craft of rope making needed for the sailing ships of the time. In 1780 it was laid out as a street and became a fashionable place of residence. Houses rapidly gave way to shops, however, and over the next 150 years this street became one of the most fashionable and exclusive shopping areas outside London, frequently compared to Bond Street.

The **Lyceum** was designed by **Thomas Harrison of Chester (1744-1829).** It was built between 1800 and 1802

Lyceum

to house the **Liverpool Library,** which was the first circulating library in Europe, founded in 1757. The accommodation included a fine newsroom and coffee house facing onto Waterloo Place. This, and the library itself, had separate entrances from the recessed Ionic portico fronting Bold Street. However, membership of the library and coffee house was soon separated. The latter developed and expanded to become the **Lyceum Gentlemen's Club** which eventually took over the whole building. After over a century and a half in the building the club moved to other premises in the City Centre in the 1970's.

The **George Henry Lee department store,** at the junction of Church Street and Parker Street, occupies a site that was formerly the residence of **Dr. James Currie (1756-1805)** a doctor, humanitarian and man of letters.

CLAYTON SQUARE; SARAH CLAYTON; OWEN OWEN; ST. JOHN'S MARKET.

The original **Clayton Square** was laid out between 1745 and 1750 by **Sarah Clayton (1712-1779),** a colliery owner and coal merchant. **Parker, Houghton** and **Leigh Streets,** which are situated nearby, were laid out at the same time and named after members of the Clayton family. Sarah Clayton

Sarah Clayton

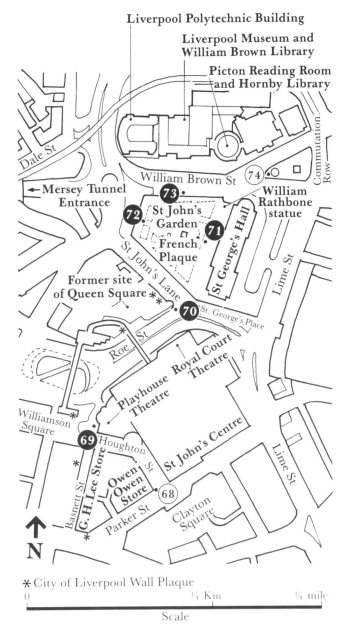

Liverpool Polytechnic Building

Liverpool Museum and
William Brown Library

Picton Reading Room
and Hornby Library

William Brown St

Mersey Tunnel
Entrance →

73

72 St John's
Garden

William
Rathbone
statue

71

French
Plaque

Former site
of Queen Square

St John's Lane

St George's Hall

Lime St

70 St. George's Place

Roe St

Playhouse Royal Court
Theatre

Williamson
Square

69 Houghton St

Owen
Owen
Store

St John's Centre

Lime St

68

G.H.Lee Store

Basnett St

Parker St

Clayton
Square

N

✻ City of Liverpool Wall Plaque

0   ¼ Km   ¼ mile

Scale

declined, and by the end of the eighteenth century was the hub of the town's vice and crime.

The north side of the square was originally occupied by the **Theatre Royal** which was built in 1772 and closed as a theatre in about 1884.

In the early 19th century a popular actor at the theatre was **Julius Brutus Booth**. He left Liverpool for America in 1821 and later his younger son, **John Wilkes Booth,** assassinated President Abraham Lincoln at Ford's Theatre, Washington in 1865.

The **Playhouse Theatre** was built in 1865 as the Star Music Hall. It was reconstructed as a repertory theatre by **Professor S.D. Adshead** in 1911 and houses Britain's oldest repertory theatre company. Many famous actors and actresses have appeared here, including **Cecil Parker, C. Aubrey Smith, Diana Wynyard** and Liverpool-born **Rex Harrison.** Both **Noel Coward** and **Gertrude Lawrence** appeared in a play here as children.

Playhouse Theatre

George Henry Lee's store was started by H. B. Lee as a straw plait business in Hunter Street. He moved to Basnett Street in 1830 and later in 1853 went into the retail business. His sons George Henry Lee and Henry Boswell Lee junior took over in 1859. In the early 20th century the store was taken over by Gordon Selfridge and eventually sold to the John Lewis Partnership in 1940.

had her house built in the square just opposite from where Owen Owen's department store now stands. After visiting Bath and admiring its architecture, much of it designed by John Wood the Elder, Sarah Clayton recommended that he be appointed architect for Liverpool's third Town Hall, which stands at the north end of Castle Street.

Half of the original Clayton Square disappeared when **Owen Owen's store** was built in the 1920s. **Owen Owen** was the son of a Merioneth farmer, and founded the firm after he came to Liverpool in 1868. He opened his first shop in London Road.

St. John's Centre, built in the 1960s, contains the market which was originally housed on part of the Centre's site at ground level in a glass and cast iron structure designed by John Foster senior.

WILLIAMSON SQUARE; JOHN WILKES BOOTH; PLAYHOUSE THEATRE; GEORGE HENRY LEE.

Williamson Square was built by the **Williamson family** in the mid eighteenth century and was a select place of residence. Its founder published the Liverpool Advertiser. Gradually, the square

WILLIAM ROE; FALL WELL; RICHARD BURTON; WILLIAM EWART, M.P.; ST. GEORGE'S HALL.

Roe Street takes its name from **William Roe,** a merchant who lived in a house overlooking Queen Square. He had a fine garden, with a fountain fed by a conduit from the Fall Well, which sprang from a site now occupied by the Royal Court Theatre. This well was one of the principal water sources for the town until the 1790s.

The **Royal Court Theatre** was built in the 1930's and has hosted many interesting productions. **Richard Burton** made his first professional appearance here in 1943 in a production entitled *'The Druid's Rest'.*

On, or in a street adjacent to, Roe Street was the birthplace of **William Ewart, M.P. (1798-1869),** a pioneer advocate of public libraries.

Looming high above St. George's Place is the south front of **St George's Hall.** A sculptured frieze was originally located in the pediment entitled *'Britannia with Commerce and the Arts'.* It was designed by **Professor C. R. Cockerell** with help from the sculptor **Alfred Stevens.** It had to be removed in the late 1940's as the stone was in a dangerous

state. The Latin inscription below the pediment reads: *'Free citizens have here dedicated a place for Arts, Laws and Councils.'*
See Marker 1 for St George's Hall.

ST JOHN'S GARDEN; FRENCH PRISONERS OF WAR; WILLIAM RATHBONE; THE RATHBONE FAMILY.

St John's Garden takes its name from St John's Church and churchyard which once occupied the site. The cemetery, containing approximately 27,000 bodies, was closed in 1854. At the end of the 19th century, in order to improve the prospect of St. George's Hall and the adjacent civic buildings, the area was laid out as a terraced garden. The scheme was designed by **Thomas Shelmerdine,** the City Surveyor, and opened to the public in 1904. The garden contains a dazzling array of sculpture by some of the best Victorian and Edwardian sculptors.

During the Napoleonic Wars, many **French** sailors were captured by the Royal Navy, and even more by privateers. They were brought back to Liverpool and incarcerated in Liverpool Gaol near St. Nicholas's Church on the site of what is now Tower Building. At one time 4,000 **French** prisoners of war were housed there, and many occupied their time making a variety of goods and novelties to sell. After the Peace of Amiens in 1802, 1,100 were liberated from the Gaol and returned to their homeland. Many prisoners, however, died in the ghastly conditions of the prison and were buried here when it was St John's Churchyard. At the base of the semi-circular retaining wall, just by this Marker at the lower level, a plaque in French and English can be found erected by the **French Government.** It states:

'To her sons who died in captivity in Liverpool 1772/1803 and whose bodies lie in the old cemetery of St. John the Baptist. France ever grateful.'

The sculptured figure in the north east corner is of the **sixth William Rathbone (1819-1902).** The sculptor was **George Frampton.** Rathbone was a member of the distinguished Liverpool dynasty of social reformers. He was an M.P. for nearly 30 years and was one of the founders of Liverpool University. He also pioneered District Nursing in Liverpool and nationally. This interest in nursing was sparked off by the need to employ a nurse to ease his wife's ill health, and it was then that he realised that the less well off had similar problems with sickness. He consulted and became a friend of **Florence Nightingale,** who had a high regard for him. On his funeral wreath she wrote: *'One of God's best and greatest sons'.*

The sixth William Rathbone

His youngest daughter, **Eleanor Rathbone (1872-1946)** worked hard for women's rights. An M.P. from 1929 to 1946, she was largely responsible for the introduction of family allowances in 1945. She was also much concerned with the plight of refugees.

The first **William Rathbone** to come to Liverpool was the **second** of that name. He came from Gawsworth, near Macclesfield, some time before 1730. He became a merchant, a shipowner and a Quaker. His son, the **third William (1726-1789),** strongly opposed the slave trade, as did the **fourth William (1757-1809).** In 1784 *'Rathbones'* brought to Liverpool the first consignment of American cotton ever landed in England – a landmark for Liverpool and Lancashire.

The **fifth William (1787-1868),** a Unitarian in later life, also had great moral courage, and was a dedicated opponent of electoral corruption.

MERSEY TUNNEL.

To the west is the main entrance to the **Mersey Road Tunnel** designed by **J. A. Brodie,** the City Engineer, with **Sir Basil Mott** the consultant engineer, and **Herbert J. Rowse** the consultant architect. Construction commenced in 1925 and the project was opened by **King George V** on 18th July 1934.

The tunnel is 3.4 kilometres (2.13 miles) long, 1.1 kilometres (0.73 miles) of which are under the river. The internal diameter of the circular tunnel is 13.4 metres (44'), with the roadway located half way up the cross section. The tunnel lies approximately 10 metres (33') below the river bed in solid rock. Just before the tunnel opened to traffic, it was made available for a charity walk at a price of sixpence per head. A number of people expressed surprise that there were no portholes to view the fish!

The entrance to the tunnel, designed by **Herbert J. Rowse,** is in Portland stone, with Egyptian art deco ornamentation. Two lodges in the form of triumphal arches are also in the art deco style.

LIVERPOOL POLYTECHNIC BUILDING; LIVERPOOL MUSEUM AND WILLIAM BROWN LIBRARY; PICTON READING ROOM AND HORNBY LIBRARY; LIVERPOOL POTTERY.

William Brown Street was named after the wealthy merchant who paid for the William Brown Library and Museum. It was formerly called Shaw's Brow, after a mayor who owned some properties on the site. It connected the road from Prescot and London to Dale Street.

The **first building** at the west end of the street is now part of **Liverpool Polytechnic.** It was designed by E. W. Mountford and opened in 1902. It is in the Edwardian imperial style with sculpture by **F. W. Pomeroy.** On the eastern pediment there is a symbolic figure of *'Liverpool',* holding a globe and sceptre supported by figures depicting the city's commerce and industries. On the western pediment, *'Minerva'* represents the wisdom of the city, presiding over the education of the community.

The next building is the **Liverpool Museum and William Brown Library.** Designed by **Thomas Allom** and opened in 1860, the building was constructed as a library, and to house the 13th Earl of Derby's natural history collection which he bequeathed to the town in 1851. The proposal to build caused a controversy. **William Brown** stepped in and offered to pay the cost. His offer was accepted and the building eventually opened amidst much celebration.

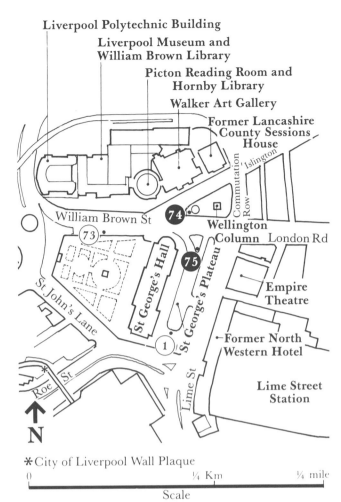

Liverpool Polytechnic Building
Liverpool Museum and William Brown Library
Picton Reading Room and Hornby Library
Walker Art Gallery
Former Lancashire County Sessions House

William Brown St.
Wellington Column
Islington
Commutation Row
London Rd.
St George's Hall
St John's Lane
St George's Plateau
Empire Theatre
Former North Western Hotel
Lime St.
Lime Street Station
Roe St.

N

✳ City of Liverpool Wall Plaque

0 ¼ Km ¼ mile
Scale

Sir James Picton

Liverpool Museum and William Brown Library

The **Picton Reading Room and Hornby Library** is the next building in the group. The circular reading room, by acting as a *'hinge'*, performs a useful civic design function in changing the direction of the frontages. It was nicknamed *'Picton's Gasometer'* after **Sir James Picton,** the Liverpool architect and historian who, as Chairman of the Libraries and Museums Committee, laid the foundation stone. Designed by **Cornelius Sherlock,** the building was opened in 1879 and is modelled on the British Museum Reading

Room. It was the first public building in Liverpool to have electric lighting.

In the mid 18th century there was a flourishing pottery industry here, and in many parts of Liverpool. Over 20 small businesses were making earthenware and porcelain in Old Haymarket, William Brown Street, St. Anne Street, Brownlow Hill, Copperas Hill, as well as Tithebarn Street, Duke Street and Park Lane. Pottery of a rough kind for tobacco pipes, bricks and tiles was made in the 17th century. Porcelain manufacture started in 1755 and was produced by eight manufacturers for the next 50 years. Competition increased from Staffordshire and the industry declined at the beginning of the 19th century. The Herculaneum Pottery Company by the South Docks continued until 1840 when the expanding docks system and Staffordshire competition closed it down.

WALKER ART GALLERY; MUSEUM OF LABOUR HISTORY; WELLINGTON COLUMN; STEBLE FOUNTAIN; COMMUTATION ROW.

The **Walker Art Gallery** was paid for by Sir Andrew Barclay Walker, the wealthy brewer, a public appeal having met with considerable opposition. The building, designed by **H. H. Vale,** was opened by Sir Andrew in 1887. Flanking the entrance are statues of *'Raphael'* and *'Michelangelo'* by **Warrington Wood.** The figure above the portico is not Britannia, but Liverpool personified as a majestic matron wearing a civic crown wreathed in laurels. She holds a ship's propeller in her left hand and the remains of a trident in her right. She is seated on a bale of cotton.

Four friezes on the building portray local events. Starting from the west, the Duke of Edinburgh is shown laying the foundation stone of the gallery, next is Queen Victoria who visited Liverpool in 1851, the third frieze shows King John granting the first charter to the burgesses of Liverpool, and finally King William III is depicted embarking at Hoylake for Ireland in 1690.

During the 18th century a Mr Gibson set up a tavern and tea garden in this area. In the garden he built an eight storey high tower, with a public observation deck at the top to view Liverpool. The venture was not a commercial success and the tower became known as *'Gibson's Folly'*. The **Museum of Labour History** now stands on the site of Gibson's Folly. The building was originally built as the **Lancashire County Sessions House** and was opened in 1887. The architects were **F. and G. Holme**.

The **Wellington Column** was inaugurated in 1863 and was designed by **George Anderson Lawson** of Glasgow. It is an exact replica of the Melville Monument in Edinburgh. The column is 40 metres (132') high, and it is said that the statue of the Duke is cast in metal from guns captured at Waterloo. The four sides of the plinth contain reliefs, the southern one depicting the *'Grand Charge'* at Waterloo.

The **Steble Fountain,** designed by **W. Cunliffe,** was erected in 1879. The bronze centrepiece contains figures representing the four seasons. It was the gift of Colonel R. F. Steble, who was Mayor of Liverpool from 1874 to 1875. On the retaining wall to the north east of the fountain, the Board of Trade Standard Measurement Table may be found, marked out in bronze pegs. This will become a museum piece when metrication is completed but is still useful as a reference.

Commutation Row takes its name from an incident in the days of the *'Window Tax'*. The residents of the row, apparently compelled to pay for their windows, decided to make the few they had as large as possible, which led to a dispute with the Inland Revenue. The situation was resolved by a *'commutation'* or understanding, being agreed upon, hence the name.

ST GEORGE'S PLATEAU; QUEEN VICTORIA STATUE; CENOTAPH; PRINCE ALBERT STATUE; EMPIRE THEATRE; FORMER NORTH WESTERN HOTEL.

St George's Plateau has seen many important ceremonies and is used on Remembrance Sunday for the laying of wreaths at the Cenotaph. It was also the scene of an all night vigil by many thousands in December 1980 after the death of Beatle **John Lennon** in New York.

The northernmost statue is of **Queen Victoria** on horseback. The sculptor was **Thomas Thorneycroft** and the statue was erected in 1870. It is a smaller copy of one by the same sculptor that graced the main entrance to the Crystal Palace in 1851 in Hyde Park. At the time it created a controversy as it depicted a lady, and the Queen at that, on horseback and in contemporary dress. It is also of interest in that it was the first external piece of sculpture in Liverpool paid for out of the rates rather than from a public subscription.

The **Cenotaph** in the centre of the Plateau was designed by **Professor Lionel Budden (1887-1956)** of Liverpool University. The two bronze sculpted panels are by **H. Tyson Smith (1880-1972)** whose studios were in Bluecoat Chambers. One panel shows marching soldiers, sailors and airmen, and the other one shows mourners.

Detail of sculpted panel on the Cenotaph

The equestrian statue of **Prince Albert** by **Thomas Thorneycroft** was erected in 1866, five years after his death.

The **Empire Theatre** was completed in 1925 and, with over 2,000 seats, is one of the largest theatres outside London. **Morecambe and Wise** made their debut as a double act at the Empire, and the **Beatles** gave their final Liverpool performance here on 5th December, 1965.

Next to the Empire to the south and situated in front of the railway station is the former **North Western Hotel**. Opened as a 330 room hotel in 1871, the building was designed by **Alfred Waterhouse** in the French Renaissance style. The Corporation made a contribution to the Caen and Storeton stone used to face the building, as it considered the site one of the most important in the Town.

Equestrian statue of Queen Victoria

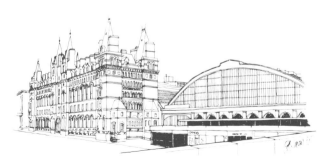

Former North Western Hotel and Lime Street Station

See Marker 1 for St George's Hall
See Marker 70 for the south facade of St George's Hall.

VISITOR INFORMATION

Merseyside Tourism Board is a private, non-profit-making company responsible for the development and promotion of tourism to Merseyside.

It produces a wide range of publications about Merseyside. Contact:
Merseyside Tourism Board
Atlantic Pavilion
Albert Dock
Liverpool L3 4AA
Tel: 0151-709 2444

First port of call for any visitor to Liverpool should be one of Merseyside Tourism Board's Tourist Information Centres:

Full range of publications and information about Merseyside. Accommodation booking service, souvenirs and postcards.
Tickets for guided tours, theatre bookings, etc.

Tourist Information Centre
Clayton Square Shopping Centre
Liverpool L1 1QR
Tel: 0151-709 3631
Open Mon-Sat 9.00 am - 5.30 pm
Sun/Bank Hols 10.00 am - 5.00 pm

Tourist Information Centre
Atlantic Pavilion
Albert Dock
Liverpool L3 4AA
Tel: 0151-708 8854
Open daily 10.00 am - 5.30 pm

Guided Tours
If you enjoyed following this Heritage Walk you may be interested in joining one of the many and varied guided walks and tours offered regularly by Merseyside Tourism Board's team of qualified MerseyGuides throughout Merseyside.
There are also daily city sightseeing and Beatles minibus tours. In addition MerseyGuides can be booked for private tours and talks at any time.
Pick up a guided tours programme at the Tourist Information Centre or call Merseyside Tourism Board on 0151-709 2444 for details of private bookings.

Other Useful Addresses

Merseytravel,
Williamson Square, Liverpool
(0151-227 5181)
For details of all public transport services within Merseyside.

Mersey Ferries,
Landing Stage, Pier Head, Liverpool
(0151-227 2660)
Services to Birkenhead and Seacombe operate approximately every 20 minutes.

Liverpool Cathedral,
St. James Road, Liverpool 1
(0151-709 6271)
Open daily 9 am - 6 pm

Metropolitan Cathedral,
Mount Pleasant, Liverpool 3
(0151-709 9222)
Open daily 8 am - 6 pm

Albert Dock,
Liverpool
(0151-709 7334)
Site open from 10 am. Shops and cafes close at 5.30 pm, restaurants and wine bars at 10.30 pm

Central Libraries,
William Brown Street, Liverpool 3
(0151-225 5429)
Open Mon-Fri 9 am - 9 pm, Sat 9 am - 5 pm

Liverpool Museum,
William Brown Street, Liverpool
(0151-207 0001)
Open Mon-Sat 10 am - 5 pm, Sun 2 pm - 5 pm

Merseyside Maritime Museum,
Albert Dock, Liverpool
(0151-207 0001)
Open daily 10.30 am - 5.30 pm
Adults £1.50, concessions 75p. Family Ticket £4.00

Walker Art Gallery,
William Brown Street, Liverpool
(0151-207 0001)
Open Mon-Sat 10 am - 5 pm, Sun 2 pm - 5 pm

Tate Gallery,
Albert Dock, Liverpool
(0151-709 3223)
Open Tue-Sun 11 am - 7 pm.
Special exhibitions: Adults £1, concessions 50p

University of Liverpool Art Gallery,
3 Abercromby Square, Liverpool
(0151-794 2347)
Open Mon, Tue, Thurs 12 noon - 2 pm,
Wed, Fri 12 noon - 4 pm

Bluecoat Gallery,
School Lane, Liverpool
(0151-709 5689)
Open Tue-Sat 10.30 am - 5 pm